The Maps That Change Florida's History

The Maps That Change Florida's History

Revisiting the Ponce de León and Narváez Settlement Expeditions

James E. MacDougald

Marsden House

The Maps that Change Florida's History:
Revisiting the Ponce de León and Narváez Settlement Expeditions

Marsden House
St. Petersburg, FL

Library of Congress Control Number: 2020944571

ISBN (hardcover): 9781735079035
ISBN (paperback): 9781735079028
eISBN: 9781735079011

Cover: Detail of the 1527 *Carta Universal* as provided in *Die Beiden Ältesten General-Karten von Amerika* by Johann Georg Kohl, 1860.

Seek, and Ye Shall Find
Matthew 7:7

Table of Contents

Appendices

Acknowledgments

THIS WORK WOULD not have been possible without the assistance of esteemed academicians who have generously provided direction, advice, and encouragement. It has been a marvelous adventure, allowing me to learn from professors of astronomy, geoscience, history, marine science, and Spanish, and to obtain guidance from those specializing in anthropology, archaeology, cartography, marine navigation, and paleography.

I am especially grateful to Professor Emeritus Martin Favata of the University of Tampa, who provided his untiring support with the translation of Spanish names and terminology, the proper use of punctuation and format, and detailed reviews of various iterations of the manuscript. Sterling Professor Rolena Adorno of Yale University, the first historian to use the 1527 Colón map in connection with research concerning the Narváez expedition, provided advice and encouragement without which this work would never have begun. Professor Emeritus Jerald Milanich of the University of Florida provided ongoing support and direction, particularly in providing guidance as to reliable reference sources. Critical knowledge about the coast of Florida as it existed in the early sixteenth century was provided by Professor Emeritus Al Hine of the College of Marine Science and by Professor Ping Wang of the School of Geoscience, both of the University of South Florida. Colonel Fred McCoy, a veteran pilot, explained the significance of the Tropic of Cancer when used in determining latitude.

Professor of Astronomy Howard Cohen of the University of Florida and Joaquim Alves Gaspar of the University of Lisbon taught me how the sun and stars were used in navigation by the early explorers. Professor J. Michael Francis of the University of South Florida provided expert translation from the Spanish of the sixteenth century. Dr. Will Michaels provided significant support in critiquing and editing the manuscript.

The guidance and assistance from those mentioned above is deeply appreciated, but I bear sole responsibility for this work.

James E. MacDougald
St. Petersburg, Florida
April, 2021

Preface

I HAVE OFTEN WONDERED why the locations of the landing sites of the earliest Spanish expeditions to *La Florida* have been generally unrecognized and unheralded. Although the first European colony established in what is now the United States occurred in 1521, it has not yet been determined where it took place. Some historians argue that Juan Ponce de León, the first governor of *La Florida*, failed to establish a settlement at all, being immediately repulsed by the native Indians when he attempted to settle somewhere on the west coast of Florida. (I refer to Native Americans as Indians, as that term was used in the chronicles of the time. With the creation of the Museum of the American Indian and after considerable debate, the terms Native American and Indian were deemed equally acceptable). Seven years later, another attempt was made, this time by Pánfilo de Narváez, who landed with four hundred men and ten women in Boca Ciega Bay, just north of the entrance to Tampa Bay. His expedition resulted in the loss of 296 of the 300 men who undertook an inland expedition, resulting in one of the greatest survival journeys ever recorded and the first book ever written about inland North America.

The two earliest European expeditions to settle *La Florida* were important events in American history yet are generally unrecognized. The Ponce de León settlement expedition is rarely referenced, and when it is, it is usually written that it probably occurred somewhere in the Charlotte Harbor area. While there is general consensus by historians that the Narváez landing site was on the shore of Boca Ciega Bay, it is marked only by a small sign in an out-of-the-way place. I had published a book, *The Pánfilo de Narváez Expedition of 1528,* in order to draw state and local attention to the importance of the Narváez expedition, hoping that it would result in wider recognition of such an important event in American history.

My study of the Narváez expedition uncovered two clues that might lead to a determination of the Ponce de León landing place. The first was the discovery of a 1527 map that indicated a "Bay of Juan Ponce." The second was the fact that Narváez, in one of his first inland expeditions, had visited an Indian village on the coast where he had found many Spanish crates and other artifacts, including iron, shoes, and cloth. I thought there might be a connection between the Bay of Juan Ponce and the discovery of cargo boxes. I had no idea that my quest would take a year, and that during that time I would learn why the Narváez expedition had failed and where Ponce de León established, for three months, the first European settlement in the United States. What I learned would change Florida's history.

CHAPTER ONE

The Search Begins

TAMPA BAY MAY have been, in the early sixteenth century, "the best harbor in the world," as Cabeza de Vaca said in his *Relación* of 1542. Tucked safely in a back corner of the huge four-hundred-square-mile bay was a smaller harbor, today known as Old Tampa Bay. While Tampa Bay may have been the best harbor, Old Tampa Bay was surely the best anchorage within it. It is totally protected from heavy winds and seas from the Gulf of Mexico and is nearly round, with an entrance at its southeastern side. Large deep draft ships of the era could sail thirty miles into the larger bay, enter a deep pass to the left, and find themselves in a serene and protected anchorage. It was the perfect place for a settlement. Yet no Florida historian has concluded that any of the earliest Spanish visitors had settled, or attempted to settle, in Old Tampa Bay.

My curiosity as to the possibility that early Spanish explorers and settlers may have "discovered" Old

Tampa Bay was piqued as the result of research I had done in connection with the Narváez expedition that landed near Tampa Bay's entrance in 1528. In 2018 my book, *The Pánfilo de Narváez Expedition of 1528*, was published. Its purpose was to consolidate and analyze all previous research by those who had attempted to determine where on Florida's west coast Narváez had debarked. His expedition had been the most disastrous of all the Spanish *entradas* in the New World, as 296 of the 300 men on the inland expedition, including Narváez himself, had perished. The four survivors had traveled more than two thousand miles over a period of eight years, finally connecting with other Spaniards near the Pacific coast of northern Mexico and then traveled another thousand miles south to Mexico City. The purpose of my book had been to firmly establish the landing place in order to encourage state, county, and local officials to in some way identify the place from which the first major inland exploration of the United States had begun. It became one of the greatest recorded survival journeys in history. One of the survivors, an African slave named Estevanico, later become the first non-native to enter what are now the states of Arizona and New Mexico. A resulting book published in 1542 by another survivor, Alvár Núñez Cabeza de Vaca, became the first book ever published about the peoples, wildlife, geography, flora, and fauna of inland North America.

In addition to a summary of conclusions of all previously published research, I had added my own analysis based on information from my personal experience sailing the west coast of Florida. I also had additional assistance from marine scientists, who helped to determine the water depths and coastal geography of Florida in the early sixteenth century. I had also included maps of various bays on the west coast of Florida, an element that was lacking in earlier attempts to identify the landing place. While the book reaffirmed historians' findings that the landing took place on the Pinellas Peninsula (somewhere in today's Boca Ciega Bay, about fifteen miles north of the entrance to Tampa Bay), it left a number of unanswered questions.

The Narváez settlement expedition had failed because Narváez had divided his forces, sending his ships northward along the coast while he led his three hundred men and forty-two horses northward along the coastline, planning to rejoin at a huge bay that he believed was nearby. They never rejoined, as there is no large bay on the Florida coast north of their landing site. The nagging questions remaining after my research were, "What had made Narváez and his pilots so certain that a large bay, extending thirty miles inland, was just to the north? Did they have a map?" Another question involved Narváez's discovery of European artifacts. Narváez, on his second inland exploration, had traveled to the shore of Old Tampa Bay and to an Indian village, where he found "many boxes from Castile," as well as other remnants of cloth, shoes, and iron. Could what he found have been remnants of the disastrous Ponce de León expedition? Ponce de León had established, or attempted to establish, a settlement on Florida's west coast seven years earlier, and its location has never been determined.

In my research of the Narváez expedition, I had found only one book that had contained reference to a map that might have been available to Narváez when he left Spain. It was contained in *Álvar Núñez Cabeza de Vaca: His Account, His Life, and the Expedition of Pánfilo de Narváez* by Rolena Adorno and Patrick Charles Pautz.[1] They provided a copy of the Gulf of Mexico portion of a 1527 map that had a heading, "Land that Pánfilo de Narváez is now going to populate." Its citation is: "Detail of Mexico, the Gulf of Mexico, and Caribbean section of the 1527 world map titled *Carta universal en*

---

1   Rolena Adorno and Patrick Charles Pautz. *Álvar Núñez Cabeza de Vaca: His Account, His Life, and the Expedition of Pánfilo de Narváez.* Lincoln and London: University of Nebraska Press. Vol. II, p. 36

que se contiene todo lo que descubr[ieron] del mundo sea fasta aora [A universal map on which is contained all that has been discovered in the world to date 1527], known as the Hernando Colón map. USLC, Geography and Map Division, Johann Georg Kohl Collection, no. 38." (Map 1). (I will refer to this map in the following text as the USLC Colón map.) Adorno and Pautz had written that since the map was dated 1527 and Narváez had left Spain in June of that year, there is no assurance that he would have seen the map before he left but that the information contained on it would certainly have been available to him. In examining the map with a magnifying glass, I saw that it contained several toponyms on the west coast of Florida, one being b. de Juan Ponce, perhaps the site of Juan Ponce de Leon's settlement attempt of 1521.

Since the five hundredth anniversary of the Ponce de León settlement expedition would occur in 2021, I determined that the timing for further research was certainly appropriate. I was haunted by the idea that Narváez may have found remnants of the Ponce de León expedition, and that such an obvious connection between Narvaez's discovery and the Ponce de León expedition had been overlooked. I wondered if the identification of the "Bay of Juan Ponce" on a map that might have been available to Narváez could explain why he had been so sure that a bay extending thirty miles inland was somewhere near his landing site. The failure of the expedition and the loss of 296 lives was caused solely because of his belief that the huge bay was nearby to the north . . . a bay that he never found, because it was located to his south. A number of historians have painted Narváez and his pilots as stupid or incompetent, or both, because of their search for a large bay that they never found, and their references to seeking the River of Palms or Pánuco, which were both in Mexico, by going north along Florida's coast. If they had had a map, it would explain why Narváez and his pilots had made the decisions that they had. The presence of a toponym for the Bay of Juan Ponce on the map would show that Narváez's pilots had good reason to believe that they were near a huge bay extending thirty miles inland, as indeed they were. More importantly, it might also locate the place that Ponce de León had attempted to establish a settlement. No one has heretofore been able to establish the place where Juan Ponce de León had attempted to establish the first European colony in what is now the United States, but many have written, without any substantiation, that it most likely occurred in the Charlotte Harbor area. Two questions might be answered if I could find the original full-scale map that had been partially shown in Adorno and Pautz.

My nearly year-long journey of research and discovery began with the attempt to locate the original of the map that had been reproduced in Adorno and Pautz. The Library of Congress 1527 Colón map has not been scanned and placed online. In the course of my search for the original full-scale version of the map, I found a recurring reference to an official Spanish 1527 *Carta Universal,* located at the Grand Ducal Library in Weimar, in virtually every book related to cartography of the early sixteenth century. Each reference included descriptions of 1527 and 1529 Spanish world maps in Weimar, and a 1529 Spanish world map located at the Vatican. The two maps in Weimar had been copied and published to accompany a book published in 1860, *Die Beiden Ältesten General-Karten von Amerika Ausgeführt in den Jahren 1527 und 1529,* by Johann Georg Kohl. As I acquired books on cartography relating to the early Spanish exploration of the New World, I found that virtually none attempted to show the maps; they just described them. The original maps were six feet by three feet or larger. It was impossible to shrink maps of that size into book-sized reproductions. Reducing a six-foot by three-foot map of about 2,600 square inches to a book-sized 35 or 40 square inches (less than 2 percent of its original size) makes all but the largest headings unreadable.

After extensive research, I learned that the 1526 Vespucci world map, the 1527 Colón, and two 1529 Ribero maps are the only extant official maps produced by the *Casa de Contratación* in Seville that are known to have survived. The good news was that the 1526 map is available to see online at a relatively large scale, but the bad news, once examined, was that it contained no useful toponyms on the west coast of Florida. The 1529 Ribero is available in two forms. The original is in the Vatican, and photographs of it can be enlarged and studied, but it has not been scanned at high resolution to allow enlargements of select areas. The Vatican map had been loaned by the Pope to an English cartographer, William Griggs, in 1889, and he had produced an exact copy of the map, as seen when compared to enlarged photos of the original in the Vatican. A digitized scan of the 1889 copy of the Vatican map is available at the Library of Congress. Although it is useful for study in that it can be downloaded and enlarged, allowing identification of the Bay of Juan Ponce and several other place names on the Florida west coast, the fact that it is dated 1529 would rule it out as a map that might have been available to Narváez.

The two maps that had been preserved at the Grand Ducal Library in Weimar, one dated 1527 by Colón and the other dated 1529 by Ribero, had been copied by J. G. Kohl and included with his book, published in 1860. The Weimar library has been renamed Herzogin Anna Amalia Bibliothek, and it offers online versions of the Kohl book, the original maps, and the maps provided by Kohl. The originals are quite faded, making toponyms difficult or impossible to read. Although the maps on the Anna Amalia website can be enlarged, the resolution of legends and toponyms is poor. In order for me to see the 1527 map at high resolution, I needed to locate a copy of the original Kohl book and the maps that it contained.

It is not known how many copies of Kohl's book were published. Worldcat.org, the world's largest library catalog, lists twenty-three copies in the U.S. and twenty-five in Europe, most of them at university libraries. None were in Florida. None of the libraries allowed removal of the book from their premises. Even if permission were granted to study them, the fact that they are in German presents a significant barrier, and it would be impossible to make full-scale copies of the maps. My next search attempted to find a copy of Kohl's book, including the maps, available for purchase. A search of Bookfinder.com and Vialibri.net, the largest search engines of books in the world, found that only one copy was in the hands of a private rare book dealer and was for sale. With considerable trepidation,

I placed the order for the $3,000 book, having no idea of what I would receive other than a description, a photo of the cover, and assurance that it contained two maps.

What I received was a folio-sized book written in German and consisting of about 160,000 words, all dedicated to descriptions of the 1527 and 1529 maps and the history surrounding them. Inserted at the back of the book were two folded maps. When unfolded, each of them was two feet by three feet in size. I compared them to the original 1527 and 1529 maps posted online by the Anna Amalia Library. Although the resolution on the maps was unclear in many places, I found that the shapes of the landmasses and larger (thus legible) legends were the same, providing assurance that the Kohl versions were faithful copies of the originals.

My first step was to take the maps to a firm that had the capacity to scan maps of that size at very high resolution and color. Multiple full-size prints were made, with some areas enlarged. It is from these prints that subsequent studies could be made. An enlargement of the Gulf of Mexico area was chosen for the cover of this book. It is quite likely that the map on the cover has rarely, if ever, been seen before by a Florida historian.

At last I had assembled full-sized versions of four important maps that had been created at the *Casa de*

Contratación in the early 1520s. Three were dated 1529, all were by Ribero, and all were versions of the same map. One was an enlarged version of a photograph of the Vatican map, another was the copy of the Vatican map that had been made in 1889, and the third was the copy of the 1529 Ribero map, as provided by Kohl. Only one map was dated 1527 . . . the Colón map provided by Kohl. When compared with the USLC Colón map, it was seen that the USLC map was a tracing of the original Kohl version as to coastal geographic features, but that it contained no portolan lines and that there were other minor differences.

The maps contained place names that likely would only be recognized as significant by a researcher with local knowledge of Florida. Only a Floridian familiar with the west coast of Florida might notice that a river on the map, the *Río de la Paz*, might be what is today known as the Peace River that flows into Charlotte Harbor. Close inspection of the maps revealed that latitude scales are included on both the Ribero and Colón maps.

The more I examined the maps, and the more research I did as to the latitudes, legends, cartouches, and toponyms on the maps, the more important I knew these maps were to Florida history. I commenced a year-long effort to study what historians have concluded to be the locations of places landed and routes traveled by early explorers, and to compare their findings with the two maps.

The first Spanish attempts to establish settlements in what was then known as *La Florida* all occurred on its west coast. The first was by Juan Ponce de León in 1521. It was followed by Pánfilo de Narváez in 1528, Hernando de Soto in 1539, and Tristán de Luna y Arellano in 1559. None were successful, although the Tristán de Luna settlement near present-day Pensacola lasted for two years before it was abandoned. The first permanent European settlement in what is now the United States finally took place in 1565, but on the east coast of Florida in St. Augustine. The west coast of Florida had vanquished all those who sought to conquer it.

Juan Ponce's 1521 settlement attempt was abandoned when he was wounded in battle with the Indians. The survivors had taken him to Cuba, where he died of his wounds. Historians have relied on scant written accounts to attempt to determine the Ponce de León landing place, or whether or not Juan Ponce actually succeeded in establishing a settlement at all. There has never been a scholarly consensus achieved that a settlement was established, but all agree that the Ponce de León landing likely occurred in or near today's

Charlotte Harbor. The expedition is especially worthy of recognition as it was the first European settlement, or settlement attempt, to occur in what is now the United States.

Pánfilo de Narváez's arrival on the shores of Florida seven years later was an unplanned one. He had set out from Cuba to establish a settlement on the northeastern coast of Mexico. A series of storms and strong prevailing winds forced him north to Florida. His expedition was also a disaster, costing Narváez his own life, as well as all but four of the three hundred men who had accompanied him on the inland expedition.

In 1539 Hernando de Soto landed near the entrance to Tampa Bay with a huge exploration and settlement expedition. Soto and nearly half of his men perished during their four-year four-thousand-mile journey. The survivors had built boats on the banks of the Mississippi River and ultimately reached Pánuco on the eastern coast of Mexico.

Only two small Spanish missions to the central west coast of Florida are known to have occurred after the Soto expedition. A Dominican priest, Luis Cáncer de Barbastro, waded ashore somewhere on the coast near Tampa Bay in 1549, planning to make peace with (and convert) the natives. They clubbed him to death.

In 1567, Pedro Menéndez de Avilés, who had founded

St. Augustine in 1565, came to Tampa Bay attempting to make a treaty between the local Tocobaga chief and the Calusa chief to the south. Menéndez, having achieved apparent success, returned to St. Augustine, leaving a garrison of thirty men. Less than a year later, a supply ship commanded by Pedro Menéndez Márquez arrived in Tocobaga. The Tocobaga had previously killed all but three of the Spaniards manning the garrison. Seeing the Spanish ships arrive, they killed the last three Spanish soldiers and fled. Márquez burned their village to the ground.[2]

The first settlement expedition to Florida that is reasonably well-documented is the Pánfilo de Narváez expedition that left Cuba in February 1528. Narváez headed for the River of Palms on the northeastern coast of Mexico but landed on the west coast of Florida instead. It is better known as the Cabeza de Vaca expedition and survival journey, primarily because it was Álvar Núñez Cabeza de Vaca, one of only four survivors of the inland expedition, who published a book describing it in 1542.

Historians have relied primarily on two sources in

---

2   John. E Worth. *Discovering Florida: First Contact Narratives from Spanish Expeditions along the Lower Gulf Coast.* Gainesville: University Press of Florida, 2014. p. 36

order to determine the landing site and subsequent travels of the Narváez expeditionaries. The first is the account by Álvar Núñez Cabeza de Vaca, generally known as the *Relación*. It was written for the king in 1537 and later published as a book in 1542. The second is the "Joint Report," dictated to the scribes of the Viceroy of New Spain (Mexico) in 1536 and signed by Cabeza de Vaca and the two other Spaniards who survived the expedition, Alonso del Castillo Maldonado and Andrés Dorantes de Carranza. A fourth survivor, Estevanico, the slave of Dorantes, wasn't officially recognized as having been involved in recounting their eight-year journey, although he may have helped the others in recalling people, places, and events. Although the Joint Report has been lost, a noted chronicler of the Spanish exploration and conquest of the New World, Gonzalo Fernández Oviedo y Valdés (Oviedo), summarized it in a massive work that was first published in modern times in Madrid in 1863. It is from these two primary sources, supplemented by information taken from maps, letters, chronicles, and sailing directions, that researchers have attempted to determine the initial Narváez landing site and the routes of inland and coastal explorations.

Seven different translations of the *Relación* were examined and compared. I found the translations by Martin Favata and José Fernández in *The Account: Álvar*

Núñez Cabeza de Vaca's Relación, and another by Rolena Adorno and Patrick Charles Pautz in *The Narrative of Cabeza de Vaca* (both available as paperbacks) to be virtually identical, with minor differences of little consequence, and employed them as my master versions. For a translation of the Joint Report, I relied on *The Expedition of Pánfilo de Narváez* by Gerald Theissen. For additional reference, I relied heavily on the Adorno and Pautz three-volume masterwork, *Álvar Núñez Cabeza de Vaca: His Account, His Life, and the Expedition of Pánfilo de Narváez*. It contains the original Spanish along with their translation, as well as extensive additional research concerning the expedition.[3]

It is from accounts of the Narváez 1528 expedition that the clues of location of the 1521 Ponce de León settlement site first appear. The Narváez expedition had failed because they had sought a large bay, extending thirty miles inland, north of their landing site. Narváez had sent his ships north along the coast while he and three hundred men followed the coastline in the same direction, certain that they would rejoin in the huge bay to the north. They never met again because there

---

3   More on primary reference sources for the *Relación* and the Joint Report is contained in Appendix I

is no large bay to the north of their Boca Ciega Bay landing site. Although never named in the *Relación*, the bay that they sought may have been the *Bahia de Juan Ponce*, where Ponce de León had been mortally wounded in his 1521 settlement attempt. Narváez, in his first forays inland, had arrived at an Indian village ·where he found many wooden crates of Spanish origin and a number of European artifacts that may have been remnants of the Ponce de León expedition.

Historians studying the early exploration of Florida have had to rely on books, maps, archival documents, and archaeological discoveries to do their research. Unfortunately, they have had to do it without useful maps. Although a few maps exist that were drawn in the decades during which the Juan Ponce de León and Pánfilo de Narváez expeditions occurred, they are too large to allow book-sized reproductions to provide legible details. In modern times, a few attempts have been made to display them in books about cartography, but the book-sized reduction in the scale of the maps prevents any but the largest toponyms and legends from being read.

Efforts to locate the places of the early Spanish landings in Florida have been based primarily on written accounts. The west coast of Florida presents a particularly vexing problem to those who attempt to use only written descriptions in order to determine landing or settlement sites. It is 350 miles long, lies generally north–south, and consists of a long line of barrier islands, shallow waters, and a monotonous coastline unbroken by any obvious landmarks, mountains, or promontories. There are numerous passes through which ships of the era might have sent landing parties, including two large bays, Charlotte Harbor and Tampa Bay, and many smaller ones, all lying north of Havana, where most expeditions to Florida began.

Archeologists have played a hand in attempting to find evidence of early Spanish presence on Florida's west coast, particularly in the excavation of middens and burial mounds. A large number of middens were destroyed as cities developed along the coast in the late 1800s and early 1900s; the crushed shells were used in the paving of roads or simply destroyed because they were on or near a building site. In 1993, I. Mac Perry published *Indian Mounds You Can Visit*, writing, "where thousands of Indian mounds once existed, only a few hundred remain."[4] He described 165 remaining sites along the coast, many of which have not been excavated. Many mounds have been found on the

---

4   I. Mac Perry. *Indian Mounds You Can Visit*. St. Petersburg.
     Fl: Great Outdoors Publishing Company, 1993

mainland and islands in the Charlotte Harbor and Tampa Bay area. Few artifacts of European origin have been found in the Charlotte Harbor area.[5]

Historians also use maps to attempt to compare toponyms with written descriptions in order to identify landing places and settlement sites. Maps have always presented a problem to historians, as the maps they require are almost always those that are provided in books, reduced in scale, making toponyms unreadable. The absence of large-scale maps with legible toponyms has led to theories as to several landing sites that are met by a counterclaim by another historian that another place on the coast of Florida meets the same criteria.

Large scale copies of the 1527 and 1529 *cartas universales* provided me with a significant advantage over those who had written of the Ponce de León and Narváez expeditions without reference to these maps. In my study of the Colón and Ribero maps, I recognized that additional research into the early exploration and settlement of the Indies and New Spain was required so that the toponyms and legends on the maps could be placed into proper historical and chronological context. I studied the roles that had been played by those named in legends on the maps, particularly Francisco de Garay

---

5   Adorno and Pautz, Vol. II, p. 83

and Lucas Vázquez de Ayllón, as well as the experiences of Juan Ponce de León and Pánfilo de Narváez in the exploration and conquest of the Indies before their final expeditions began.

Having completed my study, I analyzed the maps that had been drawn before and after their expeditions, placed the maps in chronological order, and closely examined the legends and toponyms contained on them. I also examined the latitudes contained on the maps and the written directions that were provided to pilots sailing to the New World in the *espejo* of Alonso de Chavez. I acquired an astrolabe and a quadrant and bought books and communicated with astronomers in learning how the pilots of the 1500s used them. The latitudes shown on the maps proved that the cosmographers and mapmakers in Seville, and the Spanish explorers who came to the New World in the mid-1520s, knew a lot more about geography and the latitudes of places in the New World than has been generally believed.[6]

To put the legends and toponyms on the maps into context with written accounts, we will first take a brief look at the coastal geography of the west coast of

---

6   More on the determination of latitude in the early sixteenth century is contained in Appendix II

Florida as it existed five hundred years ago. That can then be followed by a review of the early exploration of the Indies and the roles played by Ponce de León, Narváez, and some of the others whose names are featured on the maps. Only then can a close look at the maps drawn before and after the Juan Ponce and Narváez expeditions be placed in proper historical and chronological context and provide us with a better understanding of two expeditions that were signal events in Florida and American history.

CHAPTER TWO

Coastal Geography of the West Coast of Florida

IN MY RESEARCH of those who wrote of the early Spanish exploration of Florida, I couldn't help asking, "Were any of them sailors?" I found only one. Douglas T. Peck, a historian of early Spanish exploration, had sailed the entire route of Ponce de León's 1513 voyage, as described by Antonio de Herrera y Tordesillas.[7] His route had included only a small portion of the southwestern coast of Florida, but his description of the areas surrounding today's Charlotte Harbor and to its south is helpful in an analysis of landing places and bays suitable for anchorage, as

---

7   Douglas T. Peck, "Reconstruction and Analysis of the 1513 Discovery Voyage of Juan Ponce de León." *The Voyages of Ponce de León.* Compiled by James C. Cusick and Sherry Johnson. Cocoa, FL: The Florida Historical Society Press, 2012. pp. 83–102

we shall see. I had sailed the west coast of Florida for twelve years, sailing and anchoring in almost every bay and harbor from Key West and the Dry Tortugas to Anclote Key, just north of Tampa Bay. The west Florida coast is extremely shallow and is known for light breezes. Virtually every bay is blocked at its opening by islets and sandbars. Although the main passes can sometimes be twenty-or-more feet deep, the shoals outside of them are usually much shallower. Today, many channels have been dredged, and there are markers on either side of channels leading to bay openings. They are color-coded, with red markers on one side and green on the other, many lighted at night. There are excellent depth charts and man-made landmarks indicated on charts, such as large condos or radio towers, from which to get a bearing. None of those things guided the early Spanish pilots to the port they sought. A square-rigger of the early sixteenth century of the size required to carry settlement expeditions was at least seventy-five feet long, drew ten to twelve feet, was very heavy, and could only go generally downwind. It would be almost impossible to maneuver in light airs and could never make a sharp right or left turn entering bays or harbors, as it had to keep the wind generally behind it. I had always wanted to stay in safely deep waters, and the first thing I always looked for in an anchorage was a place protected from open seas and heavy winds. The sailors of five hundred years ago would surely have done the same.

A relatively small *nao* (ship) that came to the New World in the early 1500s was about one hundred *toneladas* or more.[8] One *tonelada* equaled about 1,600 pounds of cargo. A ship rated as one hundred *toneledas* could carry 160,000 pounds of cargo . . . eighty tons. That was just the cargo capacity and does not include the weight of the ship itself. Those ships would be difficult to move, requiring a lot of sail, and, unless being towed by the ships' crew in rowboats, almost impossible to maneuver in light airs.

A ship to the early explorers was a lifeline . . . the only way home. No captain of a ship wants to take the risk of running aground. He would never want to be anchored on open water or on a "lee shore." A lee shore is a shoreline downwind of the anchorage place. If the ship is anchored near shore, a strong wind from seaward could cause anchors to drag and then a permanent grounding. A ship at anchorage needs to be in a place protected from strong winds and heavy seas,

---

8   Clarence Henry Haring, *Trade and Navigation Between Spain and the Indies in the Time of the Hapsburgs*, p. 261

like a small bay. That's what I had always sought, and that's what any sailor, of any era, would seek. Those basic truths of sailing haven't changed since man first went to sea.

Where on the west coast of Florida is a place that a ship drawing ten or more feet could enter a protected harbor with deep water, sail well inland, and find a bay or a cove with a secure anchorage, protected from heavy seas? My personal experience as a sailor had taught me that there's only one . . . Tampa Bay.

No research concerning the early Spanish exploration of the west coast of Florida should be undertaken without first understanding the characteristics of the coastal geography of Florida. This is particularly important because there are only two large bays on the coastline, leading many historians to the conclusion that early landings, explorations, and settlement attempts must have occurred in one of the two. It appears that many historians have concluded that some of these landings occurred in or near Charlotte Harbor, likely because it is closest to Cuba. This is probably due to the fact that, when viewed on maps, both Tampa Bay and Charlotte Harbor appear to be large and navigable. My personal experience as a sailor, along with charts showing water levels inside these bays, tells an entirely different story.[9] Charlotte Harbor is extremely difficult to enter, with channel markers extending far seaward of its main opening, and even then requires maneuvering a twisting path toward the main channel. Its depth inside is about twelve to fourteen feet, on average. Douglas Peck, who sailed the area, wrote, *"Charlotte Harbor has been proposed as the harbor they explored, but that location is a large, shallow, almost landlocked inland bay with only a tortuous, winding, dredged entrance through nearly three miles of offshore shoals. It hardly justifies the name harbor."*[10] But was the coastal geography of Florida the same five hundred years ago?

Following is a brief description of the coastal geography of the west coast of Florida, written with the assistance of Professor Emeritus Al Hine of the College of Marine Science of the University of South Florida. Professor Ping Wang of the University of South Florida School of Geosciences wrote a detailed article on the subject, published here for the first time.[11]

---

9   Charts showing depths of Charlotte Harbor (Chart 11426) and Tampa Bay (Chart 11412) are too large and detailed to be reproduced in book-sized format. They are available online at charts.noaa.gov

10   Peck, p. 94

11   Ping Wang, "The West-Central Florida Coastline in 1500: How the Explorers Saw it." Appendix III

In recent decades we have learned that the west Florida coastal geography has been relatively unchanged for the past three thousand years. In the past one thousand years, sea levels have fluctuated by one foot or less. The Florida coastline of five hundred years ago, the time of the Spanish exploration of La Florida, was much as it is today, with the exception of the appearance and disappearance of many small tidal inlets. A line of barrier islands along the west-central Florida Gulf coast extends from Marco Island to Anclote Key, just north of Tampa Bay. Radiocarbon dating and archaeological discoveries have proven that many of the barrier islands were there about three thousand years ago. Although hurricanes, storms, and the inexorable impact of tidal flow have altered the locations of passes into and out of smaller bays and have eroded, eliminated, and created other barrier islands, the physics involved of tidal flows into and out of passes, carrying sand, would result in the sand being deposited, inside and outside of the passes (the terminal lobe) as the strength of the flows through the passes lessens. Only large bodies of water, trapped inside barrier islands or by surrounding geology (tidal prisms), would have enough force to generate wide and deep passes as the result of incoming and outgoing tides, storms, and hurricanes. Each of these passes would be guarded by sandbars and barrier islands just inside and outside of them, making navigation into them by large ships extremely challenging. It is therefore possible to look at today's coastal geology in order to see what the early expeditionaries encountered as they attempted to find anchorages. Large ships of the era had drafts of ten to fourteen feet. According to modern bathymetry maps and recent geophysical surveys, the very low and gradient continental shelf reaches thirteen to twenty-four feet water depth about one and a half miles seaward of the coast and then reaching water depths of twenty-five to thirty feet about six miles further seaward. Most of the inner continental shelf is nearly flat with very little local relief. While there are a few areas of deeper water within the innermost waters of the continental shelf, with the exception of the entrance to Tampa Bay, these slightly deeper waters are scattered inconsistently along the coastline and bordered by shallows.

With the exception of the deep main channel into Tampa Bay, the ships of the 1500s would have had to stay well offshore, using shallower draft vessels, such as caravels, brigantines, or small service boats, in order to reach shore. Even Tampa Bay presented a challenge. Its main channel, and the deeper bay within it, must be gained by using shallow draft ships, taking soundings, to lead the way for the larger ships. When the Hernando de Soto expedition arrived in 1539, "the armada dropped anchor two leagues [six miles] from land in four brazas [22 feet] of depth or less." The larger ships ultimately entered the bay after it had been reconnoitered by a shallow draft brigantine. "[The Governor] commanded that it should take a position on one side of the canal and the other brigantine at the other, so that ships might pass through the middle."[12]

Analysis of the two largest bays on Florida's west coast indicates that Tampa Bay would have been far more preferable as a port for early sailors, primarily because it was easier to find and had a deep and wide main channel. The westernmost headland of the Florida peninsula extends seven miles into the Gulf. It is the first land that would be spotted while sailing due north, or north-northeast, in safely deep waters from the Dry Tortugas. The Dry Tortugas lie about 120 miles north-northwest of Havana. They were first mapped by Ponce de León in 1513 and are identified on all maps drawn in 1520 and later. Using only a compass, the Pinellas headland would be relatively easy to find by first identifying the Dry Tortugas and then heading north

---

12   Clayton, Lawrence A., Vernon James Knight, Jr., and Edward C. Moore. *The De Soto Chronicles*. Two Volumes. Tuscaloosa: The University of Alabama Press, 1993. Volume I, p. 252

or north-northeast until land was sighted. Tampa Bay's entrance is twenty miles south of the westernmost point of the Pinellas headland.

Unlike Tampa Bay, what we today call Charlotte Harbor does not have a single broad and deep entrance channel. Charlotte Harbor has numerous entrance channels, but none nearly as wide or deep as Tampa Bay. Its deepest channel, Boca Grande, is narrower and shallower than Tampa Bay's and is hidden by numerous sandbars and barrier islands that extend well out into the Gulf. Its main channel would be difficult to spot from offshore due to numerous spits, islets, and sandbars. While it is almost certain that early explorers entered what is now known as Charlotte Harbor, it is likely that smaller caravels and brigantines were used, as the depths outside and inside the passes are thirteen feet or less . . . often much less. Tampa Bay would have been the easiest to find and appears to be the only bay that large ships of the era could have successfully navigated. These are practical realities that must be considered by researchers and historians who study the early Spanish exploration of the west coast of Florida.

CHAPTER THREE

Juan Ponce de León and Pánfilo de Narváez in the New World

IN 1469, ISABELLA I (age eighteen) of Castile had married her second cousin, Ferdinand II (age seventeen) of Aragon. Each was in line to inherit their thrones, which, after the deaths of their parents and with considerable political intrigue, they did. Their union as rulers of Castile and Aragon were the beginning of a united Spain. In 1492, the Moors were evicted from Spain, ending their 781 years of occupation with the fall of their last bastion, the city of Granada. In the same year, Ferdinand and Isabella appointed Christopher Columbus as Admiral of the Ocean Sea and Viceroy and Governor of all the lands that he might discover and sent him westward to find a new route to the Orient. Columbus had sailed west until he first came upon an island in the Bahamas, and then the islands now known as Cuba and Hispaniola.

He believed that he had reached "the Indies" of the Orient. He returned to Spain and reported his great discovery to King Ferdinand and Queen Isabella. They immediately sent him back to extend his exploration, and in 1493 he returned with seventeen ships and more than 1,200 people to establish settlements in the Indies. In this second expedition, he discovered numerous additional islands, one of which he named San Juan Bautista (today's Puerto Rico). One of the settlers accompanying Columbus was Juan Ponce de León.

The Spanish sought to claim the "New World" as their own. They established a line of demarcation between the territories of Spain and Portugal by obtaining a Papal Bull from Pope Alexander VI in 1493. It was formally ratified by the monarchs of Spain and Portugal in the Treaty of Tordesillas in 1494, giving the Spanish the rights to all lands that were more than 370 leagues (1,100 miles) west of the Cape Verde Islands and ceded to Portugal the rights to all lands eastward of the line. It was modified and formally approved by Pope Julius II in 1506.

With an established, if tenuous, line of demarcation between Spanish and Portuguese territories, Spain had free rein to exploit its discoveries in the New World, and it did so with gusto. In short order, the lands of the "New World" began drawing a multitude of expeditions from Spain to the new settlements in "the Indies" in search of even more islands and the mainland itself. A table of registered vessels sailing to the Indies after 1503 shows 600 ships sailing to the Indies from 1504–1521 and 426 returning to Spain during that period, leaving 174 ships in the Indies for further exploration and settlement.[13] There were also many additional ships that had sailed to the Indies between 1492 and 1504, leaving a number of them to remain in the New World for further exploration.

The islands of San Juan Bautista (later named Puerto Rico), Jamaica, Hispaniola, and Cuba were conquered and settled between 1493 and 1514. Columbus established the first settlement in the New World in what is now the Dominican Republic on the island of Hispaniola on his second voyage to the Indies in 1493, in a place he called *La Isabella* in honor of the queen. It was found unsuitable and the islands' capital was moved to Santo Domingo, named after his father, five years later. With Columbus on his second voyage were Diego de Velázquez de Cuéllar (Velázquez), Francisco de Garay, and Juan Ponce de León. All three would become famous and powerful in the years to come.

Ponce de León established the first settlement in

---

13   Haring, p. 339

Puerto Rico in 1508 and became its governor in 1509. Velázquez participated in the conquest of Jamaica in 1509, accompanied by Pánfilo de Narváez. Narváez had first arrived in the Indies at some time before 1500, as he later recounted to the king.[14]

Columbus had been stripped of his titles by Ferdinand and Isabella because of his tyrannical rule, and he died in 1506. His son, Diego, began a battle with the courts and the crown to claim his hereditary rights as the Viceroy of the Indies for himself. The conflict was finally resolved in Diego's favor when he was sent to the Indies as the new Viceroy in 1511. Ponce de León was removed from his post as governor of the island that he had first settled in 1508. He immediately sought the right to claim new lands of his own and was given the right to "discover" and govern an island known as Binini (Bimini) and other lands that he might encounter.

In 1512, Diego Columbus, Viceroy of the Indies, sent Velázquez to conquer Cuba. Velázquez took with him as his chief captain Pánfilo de Narváez and another captain, Hernán Cortés. Narváez is said to have watched as his men slaughtered hundreds of Indians

---

14   Buckingham Smith, *Relation of Alvar Nunez Cabeza de Vaca*, p. 207

in a barbarous act of cruelty that was witnessed by Fray
Bartolomé de las Casas, who wrote of his horror of the
event and became the greatest champion for Indians'
rights in the following decades.[15] When the conquest
of Cuba was completed in 1514, Velázquez, Narváez,
and Cortés were rewarded with large estates on the
island. Narváez had become Velázquez's favorite and
was appointed the second-highest official on the island.
Velázquez sent Captain Pánfilo de Narváez to Spain in
1515 to advocate for his appointment as the official
governor of Cuba.

The process for exploring and claiming lands in the
New World was a matter of routine. First the explorer
had to get a high-level appointed official to authorize
an exploration. After being authorized to undertake an
expedition, he had to find people to join it and help pay
for it. He would next "discover" a new place to claim
and then rush back to the official who had authorized
the mission, and then to the king, and ask to be named
its governor. The king was almost always willing to go
along with appointing a new *adelantado* . . . on two
conditions. The first was that the expedition had to be
paid for by the explorer or newly appointed *adelantado*

---

15   Helen Rand Parish, *Bartolomé de las Casas: The Only Way*,
      p. 18

and his associates, and the second was that the king got all of the lands and 20 percent of all the treasures that were found or taken— "the king's fifth." The king usually would, at the time of the appointment, approve land allotments for the governor and his men.

Obtaining rights to conquer and govern lands in the New World became considerably more complex in January of 1516 when King Ferdinand died in the midst of the "age of discovery." The king's son had previously died, leaving his sixteen-year-old grandson, now known as Carlos I, as the King of Aragon. He also nominally shared the throne of Castile with his mother, "Queen Joanna the Mad." She was, however, tucked away in a castillo of her own, having been declared insane by her father and was never a serious factor in the ruling of Spain. The fact that Carlos wasn't Spanish (he was born in Flanders, Belgium, and was Lord of the Netherlands and also the Duke of Burgundy) and didn't even speak Spanish caused some concern among those who had been given titles and privileges from King Ferdinand and Queen Isabella.

Narváez had arrived in Spain in late 1515, planning to petition King Ferdinand that his benefactor, Velázquez, the conqueror of Cuba, should be appointed its *adelantado*. Ponce de León returned to Spain in early 1516 to assure his continued entitlement to *La*

Florida. The death of King Ferdinand placed many new obstacles in their way. Narváez and Ponce de León, like many others, undoubtedly encountered difficulty when they learned that King Carlos traveled around his vast kingdoms and wasn't always in Spain. In his absence, other officials could issue certain rights to officials in the Indies, but they could be, and often were, later undone or changed by the king. Narváez and Ponce de León would spend the next three years in Spain. Narváez would lobby on behalf of his mentor, Velázquez,[16] while Ponce de León represented his own interests.[17]

After conquering Cuba, and while Narváez was still away in Spain, Velázquez began to send explorations to the west to discover new lands. Velázquez sent Juan de Grijalva to explore the coast and to report back any findings of gold or silver there. Not having heard from Grijalva for a considerable time, Velázquez sent a small fleet to search for him. They returned without having found him. Velázquez feared that Grijalva was lost and might not return. Grijalva, meanwhile, was actually still exploring the Mexican coast, landing in new ports, battling Indians, discovering gold, and continuing to

---

16   Adorno and Pautz. Vol. III, p. 221

17   Robert H. Fuson, *Juan Ponce de León and the Spanish Discovery of Puerto Rico and La Florida*, pp. 144–147

sail north along the Mexican coast. Not knowing this, Velázquez authorized Hernán Cortés to go look for him and explore ports in Mexico, but not to conquer or settle it, as he had not yet received permission to do so from the king. Velázquez undoubtedly would have preferred Narváez for this mission to go in search of Grijalva, but Narváez was still in Spain.

In his orders to Cortés in October 1518, Velázquez included a clause giving Cortés some latitude to operate as would best serve the interests of the king and the church. Cortés would later exploit this clause in direct defiance of Velázquez's attempts to reign him in. Cortés immediately began assembling his ships and army. Over the ensuing months, Velázquez got word that Cortés wasn't just equipping an exploration mission. He was assembling cannons, men with arquebuses and crossbows, and horses. His nervousness about Cortés's real plans heightened when Velázquez found out that Grijalva was on his way back to Cuba. One of Grijalva's ships had developed a leak and had returned in advance of Grijalva's other ships. When it arrived, word quickly got to Velázquez that Grijalva had discovered new lands, new ports, and more gold north of the Yucatán and that Cortés was obtaining information from the returning seamen. Based on this news, Velázquez sent word to Cortés that he was rescinding Cortés's authorization to search for Grijalva and explore the coast north of the Yucatán. Cortés had already spent a considerable sum of his own money outfitting his expedition and simply ignored the recall orders. He moved around to several ports in Cuba and signed on ship captains, men, and pilots from the ships as they finally returned from the Grijalva expedition.[18] By February 1519, Cortés had assembled his fleet of eleven ships and brigantines, and with his army of five hundred men, set sail for Mexico. Cortés landed in Veracruz in April of 1519. In June he cleverly established a town, Villa Rica de la Vera Cruz, held an election, and his men voted to make him its *Alcalde* (magistrate, or mayor) and also captain of the royal army, thus "legalizing" his status in Mexico.

In July 1519, Cortés received an official visitor from Cuba bearing a royal decree. Narváez had been successful in his efforts at the royal court. Velázquez had been appointed the *adelantado* of Cuba and other lands that he discovered. Velázquez had loyalists in the Cortés army, and Cortés got wind of their plan to get word to Velázquez that he was trying to take over Mexico for himself. Cortés found the plotters, arrested them, and two were executed. Cortés also immediately dispatched a ship carrying emissaries directly to his

---

18   Adorno and Pautz, Vol. III, p. 225

king, with a letter and a large quantity of gold, acting as if he had not received the royal decree from the court appointing Velázquez.[19] His letter explained that he was representing the king and God, that Cortés's army had insisted that he lead them personally, and that any powers that might be given, or might have already been given, to Velázquez should be revoked. He told his ship to sail to Spain with great speed, and they left in July. The ship stopped in Cuba, although Cortés had told them not to. Velázquez got word of an immense treasure on the Cortés ship and sent two of his own ships to capture it before they set sail, or to catch them at sea. They were unable to do so because they chased the ship in the traditional direction towards Spain. Cortés's pilots had taken a new route northward, passing between Cuba and the Florida peninsula, using the Gulf Stream, and the Cortés ship with his letter and treasure for the king was on its way to Spain.

Cortés knew that there were Velázquez loyalists among his army who might return to Cuba to expose his plans, so he beached or scuttled his ships so that a return to Cuba would be impossible. Cortés knew that

---

19 Anthony Padgen, *Hernán Cortés: Letters from Mexico*. New Haven and London: Yale University Press, 1986. pp. 3–46

if his army could share in the fabulous riches that lay in Mexico, their loyalty would be assured.

Velázquez, realizing that Cortés was operating totally independently and in violation of his orders, sent emissaries to Spain to tell his side of the story. He also determined to lead an expedition to arrest Cortés and claim his lands in Mexico. The crown's high court in the New World, the *Audiencia*, got word of Velázquez's plans and ordered him not to go. They did not want a civil war to erupt in the New World. Velázquez determined to ignore their instructions, but he was facing a new and growing smallpox epidemic in Cuba. He needed to stay on the island, preventing him from leading the expedition to Mexico himself. Fortunately, Pánfilo de Narváez had just returned from Spain and was selected by Velázquez to lead the expedition to capture Cortés and bring him to justice. The Narváez fleet of eight hundred men left Cuba in March 1520.

As the Cortés vs. Velázquez and Narváez conflict unfolded in Mexico, Francisco de Garay, now the governor of Jamaica, took steps to expand his own empire. In 1519 he sent a fleet northward to map the coastline of the eastern shore of Mexico. There has been some debate among historians as to the command of the expedition. It was most likely under the command of Diego de Camargo, as is convincingly argued by

Adorno and Pautz, but a map by a man identified as "Alonso Álvarez de Pineda," for which no historical substantiation can be found, has often been identified as the expedition leader, and the map resulting from it as the "Pineda Map" (Map 2).[20] Since the map resulting from the expedition has become known as the Pineda map, we will refer to it as such. Because of currents and prevailing winds, Camargo found himself at the southernmost tip of Florida and began following the coastline north, then west, then south, creating the first map of the coastline of the Gulf of Mexico. It was a discovery that *La Florida* was not an island but a much larger land connected to Mexico. Camargo discovered along the way the *Río del Espiritu Santo* (Mississippi River) and two ports that would later become famous, the River of Palms and Pánuco.

Camargo arrived in Veracruz and met with Cortés in 1519. Camargo attempted to reach an agreement that the lands that he had discovered north of there should become the domain of his boss, Francisco de Garay. He undoubtedly would have had to show his newly created map to Cortés in order to create a delineation of authority. It became apparent for the first time that there was a mainland connection between *La Florida*

---

20   Adorno and Pautz, Vol. III, p. 236

and the lands north of Cortés. Cortés did not agree that Garay had a legitimate claim, as Cortés held that he had already claimed the lands to the north for the king and himself. Camargo left Veracruz and sailed north and anchored in Pánuco. His ships were there for more than a month. He left a small garrison behind, evidently planning to ask permission to formally establish a settlement later. His pilots retraced their original route, sailing around the perimeter of the Gulf of Mexico, continued their mapping, and returned to Jamaica to show Francisco de Garay the map and to inform him that no agreement had been reached with Cortés. It is possible that the shape of the Gulf of Mexico soon became widely-known in the islands at the time since one could easily draw a semicircle showing *La Florida* on the east, Mexico on the west, a continuous stretch of shoreline connecting the two, with Cuba just south of the tip of Florida. This information, if not a copy of the map, may have found its way to Ponce de León some time in 1520. Garay sent his new map to the king with a letter telling of his discoveries. It indicated three regions: Florida, belonging to Juan Ponce de León; an area discovered by Garay; and an area discovered by Velázquez. Most importantly, it illustrated the then-unnamed Gulf of Mexico to be nearly round, surrounded by land to the west, north, and east, with openings to the Gulf located north and south of the island of Cuba. No boundaries were indicated on the map.

Cortés, meanwhile, had headed his forces to Tenochtitlán and entered the city, welcomed by Moctezuma, the leader of the Aztec empire. One legend has it that the Aztec emperor thought that Cortés was the god, Quetzalcoatl, while more recent studies seem to agree that Cortés's defeat of the warriors that he encountered after his landing on the coast had so terrified Moctezuma that he decided to befriend these strange men with horses, armor, crossbows, and cannons rather than fight them. Tenochtitlán, with an estimated two hundred thousand inhabitants, was one of the largest cities in the world at the time. Moctezuma's empire included an estimated four to five million subjects. In an outlying village, one of Moctezuma's subchiefs had attacked and killed some Spanish soldiers. When Cortés learned of this, he placed Moctezuma under house arrest, had the subchief and sixteen of his followers captured, brought to Tenochtitlán, and publicly burned alive. From that time until early May of 1520, Cortés ruled Tenochtitlán, while Moctezuma did as he was told. Cortés sent exploration expeditions seeking a good port and other treasures in the region. Meanwhile, Cortés's position there was weakening.

The natives of Tenochtitlán became restless as their ruler behaved as a puppet of Cortés and the Christians outlawed human sacrifices and imposed their own laws on the natives.

The Narváez fleet landed in Veracruz in April, and Cortés knew they were coming to arrest him. He moved his forces toward the Narváez army, leaving Tenochtitlán virtually unmanned. In May 1520, less than two months after Narváez had landed, a battle between the opposing forces of Narváez and Cortés took place. Narváez lost the battle, and an eye, and was captured and imprisoned by Cortés.

While Cortés had left Tenochtitlán to fight Narváez, the unrest among the Aztecs had increased. Cortés returned to Tenochtitlán, but soon thereafter the Indians revolted to reclaim their capital. Moctezuma was stoned to death by his own people. In what became known as *La Noche Triste* (the Night of Sorrows), Cortés suffered huge casualties as his army retreated from the city. Cortés would have to reconquer Tenochtitlán, this time by force of arms. The addition of Narváez's men had increased his army to more than double its previous size, but his forces had been decimated when they were driven out of the city. Narváez's troops had brought smallpox with them when they came from Cuba, and the Aztec population began suffering large losses in lives. Cortés spent the next eighteen months creating alliances with local tribes and engaging in many fierce battles as he attempted to retake Tenochtitlán.

Cortés sent another letter to the king, congratulating Carlos I on his ascension to another throne. King Carlos I, now aged nineteen, had recently added another title, this time as Carlos V, emperor of The Holy Roman Empire.[21] (His new empire was not holy, nor Roman, nor an empire, but actually a kingdom in Germany and surrounding area. The full name of his empire was "The Holy Roman Empire of the German Nation.") Cortés added his usual flattery of the king and explained to his king and emperor why it had been necessary to stop Narváez. He said that Francisco de Garay had attempted to establish a settlement at Pánuco, which Cortés had rebuffed because he had already claimed these lands for the king. He also included a map of the city of Tenochtitlán and a map of the Gulf of Mexico, obviously in a hurry to present his own version of events and to show that he knew the outline of the Gulf. It indicated that *La Florida* was a relatively small place, far, far away. It was also more detailed than the Pineda map, showing barrier islands

---

21   Padgen, pp. 47–159

along much of the coastline and names and locations of numerous rivers (Map 3).

Although the letter says that Cortés had obtained the maps from Moctezuma, the portion of the map showing the eastern portion of the Gulf of Mexico coastline, and *La Florida*, was most likely derived from the Pineda map that he had seen earlier. His accompanying letter did not state so directly, but he was obviously attempting to visually establish the fact that *La Florida* was not in any way near his area of conquest. He suggested to the king that the lands that he had conquered be called "New Spain of the Ocean Sea." To add impact to his claims and requests, he included a substantial treasure for the king.

Word of the Pineda map of the Gulf may have reached Juan Ponce de León, the nominal governor of *La Florida*, who was living in Puerto Rico at the time. It is possible that Ponce de León learned that the island that he had named and claimed, but virtually ignored since its discovery in 1513, was much larger than anyone had previously thought. It may be purely a coincidence that in late 1520 he determined that it was time to establish a permanent settlement in Florida. His small attempted settlement expedition of February 1521 was driven off by the Indians after they had landed on the west coast of Florida. He was wounded in battle and taken to Cuba on one of his ships, where he died of his wounds in July 1521. The other ship had sailed for New Spain. That left *La Florida* with no *adelantado*.

Meanwhile, in New Spain, Cortés and his allies were undertaking a siege of Tenochtitlán. His siege had begun in March of 1521. Cortés finally achieved the surrender of Tenochtitlán in September of that year. He burned Tenochtitlán, replaced its Aztec temples, and established a new city, Mexico City. Narváez remained his prisoner.

There can be no doubt that Garay and Velázquez were determined to stop Cortés, as he had established himself as the *de facto* ruler of New Spain without authorization and in direct violation of orders from his superior. The two were also strongly in competition with each other. Velázquez was legally entitled to the areas that his captain, Cortés, had conquered. Garay had received a warrant in 1519 entitling him to conquer and colonize the region north of the *Río de las Palmas*, a place that his own expedition had discovered.[22] He had named the area Amichel, and it was to be the lands between the *Río de las Palmas* and another *adelantado's La Florida*. A line of demarcation between the territories had not been resolved. Someone was sure

22   Adorno and Pautz, Vol. III, p. 258

to be named *adelantado* of *La Florida* to replace Ponce de León, and it was essential that the determination of the boundaries between the Cortés empire, Amichel, and *La Florida* be established before Cortés took over the whole continent.

In 1523 Pánfilo de Narváez was still in jail, where he had been for three years. Both Garay and Velázquez could safely assume that Cortés had become too powerful to defeat and that the king wasn't about to put an end to the steady stream of gold and silver being sent to him by Cortés. Nevertheless, the expansion of Cortés's growing empire needed to be stopped. Garay's solution was that he would personally establish a Spanish garrison at the port that Camargo had discovered. Pánuco was thought to be the northernmost reach of Cortés, and Garay was entitled to the lands north of it. In July 1523, Garay set out to establish his settlement. He missed his target and landed about 160 miles north, at the River of Palms. He ultimately found his way to Pánuco by separating his land forces from his ships, sending his ships southward and his men overland, rejoining in Pánuco. On arriving, he learned that Cortés was already established there, having replaced Camargo's men with his own. Unfortunately for Garay, Cortés had just received official word that he had been appointed Captain General of New

Spain by the king, and he had secured a letter from the king instructing Velázquez not to interfere. Garay attempted to achieve an agreement with Cortés, based on his own lawful authority to establish a settlement well to the north of the lands claimed by Cortés. He argued that he had the legitimate right to establish the settlement in his newly named Amichel, and they just needed to agree on a place for him to do so. Cortés apparently agreed that they could work something out, and the two men traveled to Mexico City to negotiate. Garay also asked Cortés to release Narváez from jail. Narváez's loyal wife, Maria de Valenzuela, had also been sending letters to Cortés, begging for her husband's release.[23] Although Garay may have been of some influence in achieving the later release of Narváez, his offer to find an acceptable boundary between his and Cortés's territories was unsuccessful. Garay suspiciously, and conveniently for Cortés, died while he was in Mexico City. Thus ended the second attempt to stop the relentless expansion of the growing Cortés empire.

Narváez was finally released by Cortés in 1524 and returned to Cuba to reunite with his wife and oversee his vast estates, which had prospered under her care.

---

23   Adorno and Pautz, Vol. III, p. 266

He undoubtedly learned that Ponce de León had attempted to settle in La Florida three years earlier and had been brought to Cuba where he had died of his wounds. In the same year, his mentor, Velazquez, died. In 1525 the king appointed Nuño Beltrán de Guzmán as *adelantado* of the area surrounding Pánuco, removing it from Cortés's control.

Since Ponce de León had died in 1521 and Garay in 1523, the lands north and west along the entire Gulf of Mexico coastline from the River of Palms to the cape of Florida required a new *adelantado*. Pánfilo de Narváez created a plan to claim those lands for himself. The demarcation between the territories formerly assigned to Garay and Ponce de León and those of New Spain was yet to be formally delineated. Narváez was the obvious choice to move up and become an *adelantado* himself.

Narváez returned to Spain in late 1525, seeking an audience with the king. He had a new plan. He would be appointed as the new *adelantado* of all of the territories that were previously the domains of both Garay and Ponce de León. His territory would be defined as all lands north of the River of Palms on the Mexican coast, extending northward and eastward to the cape of Florida.[24] He would serve the crown as royal governor. He would establish settlements and garrisons at the River of Palms and elsewhere within the limits of his vast territory, and of course remit the "king's fifth" of all the bounties that he found. This would allow the king to delineate what had been known as Amichel, and *La Florida,* from New Spain, an obviously necessary step. It took a number of petitions and a year of lobbying, but ultimately the king agreed, and on December 5, 1526, he appointed Pánfilo de Narváez as the new governor of all lands from the *Río de las Palmas* to the cape of Florida. The second attempt to establish settlements in *La Florida* would begin, not in Florida, but at the River of Palms in Mexico. Narváez likely chose the River of Palms for his initial landing because of the enormous amounts of gold that had been found by Cortés in nearby New Spain.

Neither Ponce de León's 1521 nor Narváez's 1527 expeditions would have been undertaken without first obtaining all available maps of the area that they intended to settle. They would have had maps that were in the possession of the pilots they chose to guide them to their destinations, as well as those

---

24   Buckingham Smith, pp. 208-210

from their own previous voyages, as each of them had been in the Indies for twenty-five years before their settlement expeditions began. They would also be entitled, as *adelantados* appointed by the king, to maps and sailing directions from the *Casa de Contratación* in Seville.

CHAPTER FOUR

Discovering the Maps that Change Florida's History

THE MAPS USED by Spanish pilots sailing to the Indies after 1508 were produced at the *Casa de Contratación (House of Trade)* in Seville. It had been established by Queen Isabella in 1503 as a center for administration for ships sailing to and from the Indies. In 1508, King Ferdinand had added to its role, creating a center for cosmography and piloting with his appointment of its first pilot-major, Amérigo Vespucci. The order to the pilot-major was to create a *Padrón Real* (royal pattern), a standard pattern from which all other maps must be drawn. The job of the *Casa de Contratación* was also to teach, examine, and certify the competence of pilots for navigation to the New World. In the same *cédula* (royal decree), a requirement was established that all pilots must be able to determine latitude by using the astrolabe and quadrant.[25] It was also ordered that the *Padrón Real* must include "all new lands, islands, bays, harbors, and other things worthy of being noted."[26] Pilots returning from the Indies had to submit the records of their travels to the *Casa de Contratación*, and the ship's master and pilot had to sign them and accompany them with an oath that their records fully and completely recounted their route.[27] They would also bring hand-drawn maps and sketches for use in updating the *Padrón Real*. Information flowed into the *Casa de Contratación* every time a ship returned from the Indies to Seville, and there were many. From the time the *Casa de Contratación* had been created in 1503 until Narváez left Spain in 1527, 919 ships had sailed to the Indies, and 588 had returned.[28] Although some of the ships had doubtlessly been lost, a fair estimate would be that more than 250 Spanish ships,

25   Surekha Davies. "The Navigational Iconography of Diogo Ribeiro's 1529 Vatican Planisphere" JSTOR

26   Edward Luther Stevenson. *Early Spanish Cartography of the New World.* p. 9

27   Alison Sandman. "Spanish Nautical Cartography in the Renaissance." *The History of Cartography*, Vol. III, Part 1. Chicago: University of Chicago Press. [press.uchicago.edu] Sandman, Vol. III, Part 1, p. 1104

28   Haring, p. 339

with their captains, pilots, and crews, remained in the Indies for inter-island transportation and for further exploration of the New World. They would have their own maps and sailing directions, shared with fellow mariners at the many ports where the ships with their captains and crews would meet.

The production of the *Padrón Real* presented a huge problem to mapmakers. Its scale was enormous. The 1526 Vespucci world map was three feet in height by nine feet in width, and other later world maps were of similar dimensions. Some areas of the world maps would be nearly blank, representing places unexplored at the time, or vast areas of the Pacific. Other areas, including Africa, India, and the New World, were crammed with dozens of toponyms in just a few square inches. A world map involved hundreds of toponyms, latitude scales, distances, reliable outlines of islands and landmasses, and legends describing significant places, people, and events.

In June of 1526, the Council of the Indies ordered the pilot-major to make a new *Padrón Real*.[29] In October of the same year, King Carlos ordered that the *Padrón Real* be henceforth known as the *Padrón General* and established clear rules for making and selling copies

---

29 Sandman, p. 1115

of it. In the same *cédula*, it was stated that every professional cosmographer residing in Seville could construct and sell navigational instruments and maps of the New World, provided these were first submitted to and approved by the pilot-major and pilots of the *Casa de Contratación*.[30] The cosmographers at the *Casa de Contratación* also maintained a mariner's manual, known as the *espejo,* and provided it to each pilot sailing to the New World. It provided illustrations of navigational instruments and how to use them to determine latitude using the included declination tables. It described the use of lead lines to determine depth, how to use a compass, and how to anchor properly. It also included latitudes of key ports and very specific sailing directions. An example is the sailing directions that would be found by a sailor going north from Havana to Florida (a league is about three miles): "*The south point of Florida, next to the Martyrs [Keys], is at 25 ½ degrees. It is north of the ports of Cuba, and it is 40 leagues from Havana to Matanza* [island]. *This is 18 leagues east of the point of Florida. There are many*

---

30   Henry Harrisse, *The Discovery of North America*, Henry Stevens & Son, [Paris] 1892. Microform Edition. Scholar Select. Undated. p. 267

reefs and shallows that are named the Martyrs, and to enter them you need rowboats or canoes."[31]

All maps of the Indies had to comply exactly with the *Padrón Real* (after 1526, *Padrón General*). The master version, or copies of it, at six feet by three feet, were far too large to be carried by mariners, and maps of the entire world would not have been required. It was also impossible to redraw an entire *Padrón General* every time a new port, or a new latitude, was reported to the mapmakers in Seville. Versions known as the *Padrón Ordinario,* covering just the New World portion, were prepared for pilots and were undoubtedly more current and more detailed as to navigational barriers and locations of newly discovered ports than the *Padrón General.* The *Padrón Ordinario* was required to comply exactly with the landmarks, toponyms, and latitudes of the key ports of the *Padrón General.*[32] They covered a smaller area, enabling their scale to be enlarged to allow toponyms to be read and latitudes to be measured. These maps required

---

31   Alonso de Chavez. *Transcripción, estudio y notas del Espejo de Navegantes de Alonso de Chaves.* Translated and annotated by Paulino Castañeda, Mariano Cuesta, Pilar Hernández. Madrid: Instituto de Historia y Cultura Naval, 1983. p. 367

32   Sandman, p. 1101

ample spacing between one-degree increments on the latitude scales to allow fractions of degrees to be determined. Based on the *espejo*, we know that degrees were expressed in fractions, i.e, *"Bahia de Juan Ponce está en 27 ¼ grados,"* and *"Río de San Francisco, en la costa de Brasil, está en 10 ¾ grados."*[33] Pilots took these fractional differences seriously, as each quarter degree represented approximately eighteen miles. Sandman wrote that *"Pilots throughout the century complained about latitude errors in the charts of half a degree, or less, errors that would be invisible on smaller charts."*[34] Mapmakers were constantly making maps for each of the pilots preparing to sail to the Indies, working based on a faithful duplication of the details of the *Padrón General* and adding whatever useful information that had been gained from returning pilots.[35] Since each ship's pilot was required to carry an officially approved map and *espejo*, many of each would have been produced each year. A "master version" for the Indies

33   Chavez, pp. 367 and 405

34   Sandman, p. 1097

35   Ricardo Padrón, "Charting Empire, Charting Differences: Gómara's *Historia general de las Indias* and Spanish Maritime Cartography." *Colonial Latin American Review*, Vol. XI, No. 1, 2002. p. 51

was likely created and updated as more details became known from ships returning from the Indies.

The *Padrón General* had a twofold purpose: "to provide a pattern for charts used by pilots, and to provide a reference for the ruler and later for the Council of the Indies. Thus, charts were never simply tools, but also claims about the locations and places, and so were politically sensitive."[36]

In order to determine what was known by Ponce de León before he left Puerto Rico in 1513, and to Narváez before he left Spain in 1528, it was necessary to examine any *Padrón Real* or *Padrón General* that had been produced in the years immediately before and after their departures.

I conducted a review of maps that had been produced prior to and during the period in which the Ponce de León and Narváez expeditions had occurred. An extensive review of historical and cartographical publications, and a careful study of the maps that each of them had provided or described, led to my determination that there were maps available to Ponce de León and Narváez that are generally not referenced in connection with either of the settlement expeditions.

---

36   Sandman, p. 1108

No official map produced by the *Casa de Contratación* prior to 1513 could be found, although a number of maps showing the general coastline of the Gulf of Mexico had long preceded Juan Ponce's "discovery" of *La Florida* in 1513. The general shape of the Gulf of Mexico, with Florida being separated by a large body of water from Mexico, had been known since 1500. There are a number of maps showing the Florida peninsula, the shape of the Gulf of Mexico, and the landmass connecting what was later named *La Florida* to New Spain, existing well before the Ponce de León expedition set out to "discover" Florida in 1513 (Maps 4–8).

The first map produced after the Ponce de León discovery of *La Florida* is believed to be the Freducci map (Map 9) created for Conte di Ottomano Freducci. Although undated, it is believed to have been created in the years immediately after Ponce de León discovered Florida in 1513, as the toponym *La Florida* is inscribed on the northeastern coast of Florida in the area where Juan Ponce had first discovered land.[37] This map does not show the coastline of Florida or the Gulf beyond

---

37   Osvaldo Baldacci, *Columbian Atlas of the Great Discovery.* Rome: Instituto Poligrafico E Zecca Dello Stato. Libería Dello Stato, 1992

the lower western coast of Florida. Jerald Milanich, in "Revisiting the Freducci Map: A Description of Ponce De León's 1513 Florida Voyage?" compares the similarities on the map with toponyms and sailing routes described by Herrera.[38] It appears from Professor Milanich's analysis that this is likely the first map to include the general shape of southern Florida, as well as a number of toponyms occurring for the first time on a map. The Pineda (Map 2) and Cortés maps (Map 3) had also been sent to the king and would undoubtedly have been known to the *Casa de Contratación* prior to 1521.

The search for maps drawn after the second Ponce de León expedition in 1521 resulted in a finding that there remain only five maps that were drawn at the *Casa de Contratación* during that time period. The Vespucci map of 1526 (Map 10) contained no useful toponyms on the coast of Florida. The *Carta de América y Filipinas en dos partes* by Alonso de Chavez is sometimes referred to as the "Wolfenbüttel-Spanish" map (Map 11). Although sometimes attributed with a date of 1526 or earlier, it was actually drawn c. 1532

---

38   James G. Cusick and Sherry Johnson, *The Voyages of Ponce de León: Scholarly Perspectives*. Florida Historical Society Press, 2012. Milanich, p. 110

and could not have been seen by Narváez before he left Spain.[39]

Three original *cartas universales* are known to have survived. One was drawn by Diego Ribero in 1529 and is in the Vatican. It is known as the "Propaganda" map, as it was originally preserved in the Museo Borgia of the Propaganda Fide in Rome. Although it has been photographed and printed, its huge scale makes the legends and toponyms unreadable. It was loaned in 1889 by Pope Leo XIII to a cartographer in England, William Griggs, who produced a copy that is in the U.S. Library of Congress. An enlarged photo of the Propaganda map in the Vatican was printed and compared with the Griggs version. While the original does not provide the legibility of small toponyms required, it does provide sufficient detail to confirm that the copy of the Propaganda map in the Library of Congress is a nearly exact rendition. It has been digitized, is available as a high-resolution download, and was printed at full scale.

Two other original *cartas universales* are preserved at the Duchess Anna Amalia Library (formerly the Grand Ducal Library) in Weimar. Photos of the maps have

---

39   Luisa Martín Merás. *Cartografía Marítima Hispaña: La imagen de América.* Madrid: Lunwerg Editores. [undated], p. 99

been scanned and placed online, but the maps are very faded and only the outlines of landmasses and a few (but key) legends and toponyms can be read. Both of these maps had been loaned to Johann Georg Kohl in 1860, and he had made copies of the "Americas" portion of the maps (about one-fourth of the overall originals) and provided them with a book that he published about the two maps. While these maps had been described in numerous publications and reproduced in some, all of the printed versions had been reduced in scale, resulting in toponyms so small that they could not be read.

A search for the original 1860 Kohl publication that contained the 1527 and 1529 maps ensued. A worldwide internet search resulted in the finding that only one copy of the Kohl publication was available for purchase. It was acquired by the author. It contained, as separate insertions, two large two-foot by three-foot maps that have likely not been previously seen by a Florida historian. No references to the toponyms on the west coast of Florida shown on these maps could be found in an extensive study of histories of the early Spanish exploration of *La Florida*.

Once the 1529 Ribero "Propaganda" map and the 1529 Ribero and 1527 Colón maps from Kohl's book had been scanned, digitized, printed in full scale, and compared with the originals, it became apparent that the map that had begun my search, the 1527 USLC Colón map in Adorno and Pautz, was a less-detailed tracing of the 1527 Colón map that had been produced by Kohl. Since it was a tracing of the original Kohl map, it was eliminated from further study.

The result was that three large-scale maps containing toponyms on the west coast of Florida were available for detailed study. Unfortunately, the name of the person who actually drew the 1527 map is not included on the map. Hernando Colón was the pilot-major at the time, while Diego Ribero was the chief cosmographer.[40] Although some cartographers have attributed all three of the maps to Ribero, I will refer to the 1527 map as the Colón map in order to avoid confusion in describing differences between them.

- The Ribero *Carta Universal* (1529) "Propaganda" Map (Map 12) *Carta Universal en que Se contiene todo lo que del mondo Se ha descubierto fasta agora: hizola Diego Ribero cosmographo de Su magestad: Año de 1529. ẽ Sevilla: La qual Se devide en dos partes conforme A la capitulacion que hizieron los catholicos Reyes de españa, y*

---

40   Edward Wilson-Lee, *The Catalog of Shipwrecked Books*, p. 272

elrrey don Juan de portogual En Tordesillas: *Año de 1494.* Described by the Library of Congress as "The second Borgia map by Diego Ribero, Seville, 1529. Reproduced from the original in the Museum of the 'Propaganda' in Rome. One map on two sheets 61 x 79 cm [24" x 19"] and 61 x 66 cm [24" x 26"]." The original had been loaned by Pope Leo XIII to W. Griggs in London, and he had produced this copy in 1889. It was downloaded at high resolution. The final print size of the America and Pacific portion (half of the total map) was printed at a larger scale than the original, at 23" x 30".

• The Ribero *Carta Universal* (1529) (Map 13) *Carta Universal en que se contiene todo del mundo se ha descubierto fasta agora, hizola diego Ribero cosmographo de su magestatd ano de 1529.* Also known as the 1529 Weimar map. The Americas portion, representing a quarter of the map, had been reproduced by Kohl in his 1860 publication *Die Beiden Ältesten General-Karten von America.* The book and the included map are in the personal collection of the author. The map is folded into four sections, each approximately 13 ½" x 18". It was scanned, digitized, and printed at its full scale of 27" x 36".

- The Colón *Carta Universal* (1527) (Map 14) *Carta Universal en que se contiene todo lo que en el mundo se a descub(ierto) fasta aora. Hizola un cosmógrafo de S.M. Anno MDXXVII.* Also known as the 1527 Weimar map. The Americas portion, representing a quarter of the map, had been reproduced by Kohl in his 1860 publication *Die Beiden Ältesten General-Karten von America.* The book and the included map are in the personal collection of the author. The map is folded, in four sections, each approximately 13 ½" x 18". It was scanned, digitized, and printed at its full scale of 27" x 36".

A Comparison of the Maps

The maps differ visually in immediately apparent ways. The Ribero Propaganda map has one Papal escutcheon and two coats of arms at the lower border, while the Weimar version of the Ribero has none. The Colón map much more accurately depicts the shape of Florida than the Ribero maps. The Yucatán on the two Ribero maps is shown connected to the mainland, while the Colón by Kohl shows it as an island. The Colón map also substantially elongates the Gulf of Mexico. All three of the maps, when enlarged, provide sufficient detail to enable legends and toponyms in the areas surrounding the Gulf of Mexico to be read and compared. Each map is about one thousand square inches when printed. The entire Florida peninsula occupies only two square inches (two tenths of one percent) of the area of the maps, requiring the use of a magnifying glass in order to read the toponyms. Once scanned and digitized, that area was enlarged and printed, allowing a close examination of relevant portions of the maps. Once the maps had been printed, side-by-side comparisons were made. Numerous legends and toponyms throughout the Americas were found to be different when the maps were compared.[41]

Though generally not mentioned by cartographers who have written about these maps, all the maps have latitude scales at the margin or in the interior. In the few instances that maps or portions of them have been included in publications, the latitude indicators have

---

41 A general overview of the differences in the toponyms, legends, and illustrations on these maps is contained in Appendix IV.

been cropped when the copy was made or are in such small scale relative to the rest of the map that they cannot be seen. Only by actually viewing a map at close to its original size can the latitude scales be seen. The 1527 Colón and 1529 Ribero maps are nearly identical at the margins. The portolan lines vary slightly, as do some of the shapes of landmasses. The Colón and Ribero maps are clearly not duplicates, but it appears that a common underpinning, latitude scales, was used by the mapmakers.

The discovery that the 1529 Ribero maps had been drawn in 1526

The Ribero maps dated 1529 have bold headings on the landmass above the northern coastline of the Gulf of Mexico, identifying the area as *Tierra de Garay* (Maps 15 and 16). Francisco de Garay had in 1519 originally received permission to settle the lands for one hundred leagues north and westward along the coast from Pánuco but had died in Mexico City in 1523 at the time of his meeting with Cortés. His territory was later granted to Narváez (along with Ponce de León's *La Florida*) in December 1526. Why would a 1529 map attribute Narváez's territory to Garay?

The 1529 Ribero map presented in Kohl contains

a legend, *Tiera de Garay en toda esta costa y la del liçenciado ayllon y latierra de estevan gomez no se espera de allar oro como en nueva españa por estar muy desviada del tropico,* translated by Professor J. Michael Francis of the University of South Florida as, "Land of Garay. Along this entire coast and that of the Licentiate Ayllón and the land of Esteban Gómez it is not anticipated that gold will be discovered as it has been in New Spain because [these lands] are so distant from the Tropic." The Ribero Propaganda map contains the same identification of the lands of Garay.

The Ribero maps both contain additional bold headings identifying the *Tierra de Ayllón.* Lucas Vázquez de Ayllón had received letters patent from the king to settle on the coast of present-day South Carolina in 1523. He had finally established his colony in mid-1526. He died, and his settlement was abandoned, later that same year.[42] The legend on the Ribero/Kohl map states, *Tiera de Ayllon el qual la descubrio y bolvienodola a poblar porque es tierra muy dispuesta para dar pan y vino y todas las cosas de españa fallecio aqui de dolençia,* translated by Professor Francis as, "Land of Ayllón, which he discovered and returned to settle because it is land well-disposed to produce bread (wheat) and wine

---

42   Harrisse, p. 208

and all things from Spain; [Ayllón] died here from disease."

The 1527 Colón map (Map 17) eliminates the bold headings for the lands that had been labeled on the 1529 Ribero maps as *Tiera de Garay* and *Tiera de Ayllón*. Over the northern coast of the Gulf of Mexico is written instead, "Land that Pánfilo de Narváez is now going to populate." The Colón map has a small toponym in red next to a river on the coast near today's South Carolina: *"tierra del licencíado ayllon."* On the coast west of the Florida panhandle, also in red, is a small toponym: *"donde aqui descubrío fr de garay."* Garay and Ayllón had gone from headlines on the Ribero maps to footnotes on the Colón map.

It made no sense to have a 1527 Colón map containing the legend, "Land that Panfilo de Narváez is now going to populate," and a Ribero map dated two years later identifying the same lands with a bold heading, *Tiera de Garay*. Diego Ribero had been the "Cosmographer and master of making charts" since 1523.[43] Ribero would not have produced a map in 1529 with incorrect identification as to the *Tiera de Garay*. Ribero certainly knew in 1529 that Garay had died in 1523 and that Narváez had been

―――――――――

43   Haring, p. 35

awarded the governorship of those lands in December 1526.

As I inspected the maps, I noticed other differences. The Ribero maps have many legends and cartouches, while the Colón has none. Both Ribero maps contain beautifully detailed drawings of the astrolabe and quadrant with highly specific instructions in their use, as well as hundreds of toponyms along the South American and African coasts. The Asia/Pacific portion of the Propaganda map is further enhanced, covering virtually every inch of known landmasses with names of countries, illustrations of mountains and deserts, and colorful drawings of birds and animals. On the "Americas" portion of the Ribero maps are twelve lengthy and detailed legends and cartouches from five to fifteen lines each, describing people, places, and events. The Ribero maps could not have been finally completed and dated until all of this artwork and additional information had been added, and that would have taken a considerable period of time after the geographical elements of the map were drawn. The Ribero maps were obviously "presentation" maps and would therefore ultimately be dated upon their completion and not on the date they were begun. They would be dated 1529 because that is the year they were completed, and, I believe, the year that the Propaganda version was prepared for the Marquis Lorenzo Leone Chigi, the richest man in Rome and banker to the Pope. It may have been given by Chigi to Pope Clement VII, thus gaining its place in the Vatican collection.[44]

Based on the Garay legends above the northern coast of the Gulf on the Ribero maps, it can be determined that the Ribero maps had to have been drawn before Narváez was given the right in December 1526 to conquer and govern the lands that were previously the province of Francisco de Garay. This would date the geographic representations on the Ribero maps to 1526 or earlier. The Ribero *Carta Universal* is actually older than the 1527 Colón map. It is quite likely that the Ribero "1529" map was the official *Padrón Real* as it existed in late 1526 or early 1527, replaced by a new *Padrón General* on orders from the king in late 1526. The original, and now obsolete, *Padrón Real* had apparently been heavily decorated for later presentation in 1529.

That this difference has gone unnoticed is perhaps best explained by the fact that historians have had to rely on descriptions of maps, rather than seeing them, or portions of them, at a scale that allow toponyms to

---

44   See Appendix V for a more detailed analysis of the Chigi attribution.

be read. The largest versions of the Colón and Ribero maps appear in Baldacci's *Columbian Atlas of the Great Discovery*.[45] Even though shown on two-page spreads, the cartouches, legends, and toponyms on the maps are unreadable. Baldacci translated all of the cartouches on the 1529 maps relating to territories assigned, including the *Tierra de Ayllón* and the *Tierra de Garay*. He did not note that the 1527 map contained a heading, *Tierra que aora ba apoblar panfilo de narbaes*. It cannot be seen on the map as presented in the book. He may have lacked the knowledge of the dates of the assignments of territories to Garay, and later to Narváez, and that those territorial assignments had considerable significance as to the dating of the maps. He and his fellow cartographers likely had no idea that these details on the maps would be of huge significance to those studying *La Florida*, especially to those seeking information as to what Narváez knew about geography and place names of Florida's west coast before his expedition began, or where the Bay of Juan Ponce was located.

Ricardo Padrón had found the 1529 Ribero/Kohl map at the Library of Congress and had included a copy in his paper about Spanish maritime cartography,

---

45   Baldacci, pp. 163 and 165

published in 2002.[46] It, like the versions of the Kohl maps produced before and after his article, reduced a two-foot by three-foot map to five-by-seven inches, making only the largest legends legible. He did not mention any toponyms on Florida's coast, as his article was focused on cartography, not on Florida history.

The most important thing learned from the Ribero maps professing to represent "A universal map on which is contained all that has been discovered in the world to date in 1529" is that neither of them did. The Ribero maps were both produced at the same time. The "Propaganda" map had been extensively, artistically beautified for presentation, and the Kohl version is a near duplicate as to geographical features, toponyms, cartouches, and artistic enhancements but is somewhat less ornate. The map's ornamentation had been produced over a period of time, during which the legends and toponyms that had been inscribed early in their production had been left unchanged. They appeared to represent the world as it was known in 1529, but they didn't. They represented the world as it was known in 1526.

---

46   Ricardo Padrón, "Charting Empire, Charting Difference: Gómara's *Historia general de las Indias* and Spanish Maritime Cartography." *Colonial Latin America Review*, Vol. XI, No. 1, 2002. pp. 53–55

The Maps Shed New Light on the Ponce de León and Narváez Expeditions

The toponym for the Bay of Juan Ponce on the Ribero and Colón maps, and the indication of its latitude, led to a need to re-examine long-held theories that the Bay of Juan Ponce was in or near present-day Charlotte Harbor. This examination also required a review of maps known to have been drawn after 1527, particularly the maps and accounts related to the Hernando de Soto expedition of 1539, as they also reference the Bay of Juan Ponce. It also required a study of latitudes as shown on the maps and in the Chavez *espejo* in order to determine if correct latitudes were indicated on either or both and if latitude indications in the *espejo* were the same as indicated on the maps.

Since the Ribero maps are dated 1529 and have been believed to have been drawn in that year, they have been overlooked as relevant to the studies of the Pánfilo de Narváez expedition that left Spain in 1527. Recognition of the fact that the Gulf of Mexico area of the Ribero maps were drawn before Narváez left Spain, and before the Colón map was drawn, invites close inspection of the toponyms on the Ribero and Colón maps, particularly concerning any differences between the two. Narváez would have taken a great interest in a proper identification of his territory on a map. Since the lands that he was entitled to govern extended from the River of Palms on the northeastern coast of Mexico to the Cape of Florida, he would have had a keen interest in the entire southern boundary of his territory, which was the Gulf of Mexico coastline from Las Palmas to the Cape of Florida. He certainly would have seen the detailed geographic representations found on the Ribero and Colón maps and the latitudes that they contained. This information would surely have been made available, and copies provided, to Narváez and his pilots before they left Spain.

The fact that Narváez had maps identifying many ports and rivers along the entire Gulf coast requires a re-examination of his expedition. The availability of maps to him and his pilots explains why he sailed to Florida when he was unable to reach Havana, why he believed that he was near a huge bay, and where in Florida he intended to go. It also explains why he made the decision to split his ships from his land forces, seeking a better port to the north, and why he had built boats to try to reach Pánuco.

The maps also identify the location of the Bay of Juan Ponce and represent the first time this bay is named on maps. Of the fifty-three coastal toponyms shown on the Colón map from the tip of Florida to the Yucatán, the Bay of Juan Ponce is the only place named as a bay.

Since the Ribero and Colón maps were drawn five to six years after the Ponce de León attempt to establish a colony had been repulsed, they would likely represent a location as reported by those returning from the ill-fated expedition. The best clues as to the location of the Bay of Juan Ponce would likely be found with the help of the toponyms and latitudes indicated on the maps.

CHAPTER FIVE

Examining the Colón and Ribero Maps and Latitudes

THE DISCOVERY THAT the Colón and Ribero maps included latitude scales led to additional research to determine if the latitudes on the charts were correct and to note any differences between the maps. The maps all had latitude degree scales in one-degree increments. All of the maps contain a solid line at the Tropic of Cancer. The Tropic of Cancer is drawn on maps at 23.5° as the place at which the sun is directly overhead at noon on the Summer solstice (June 21). To determine latitude from the sun's location at noon at other times of the year, declination tables were provided in the *espejo* to enable pilots to make the appropriate adjustments. The Tropic of Cancer line on all three maps crosses just north of Pánuco, the destination often referred to by the Narváez land expedition.

The latitude indicators were shown at the margins

of the maps. In order to accurately trace the latitudes indicated on the maps to selected toponyms contained on them, high resolution enlargements of the maps were printed. The Caribbean area portions of the maps were enlarged to a scale large enough to allow a line to be inscribed across the charts at one-degree increments. Lines were traced across them to determine the latitudes indicated for the Bay of Juan Ponce, the *Río de la Paz*, and Pánuco. Also selected for comparison were places that would have been well-known and would be expected to have a reliably established latitude: Santo Domingo on Hispaniola, the port of San Juan (Puerto Rico), and Villa Rica (Veracruz) in New Spain. All maps have the Tropic of Cancer shown as a dark and solid line on the map, and this was used as a baseline from which to determine the general accuracy of latitudes indicated on the maps.

Latitudes shown on maps could then be compared with those in the Chavez *espejo* and with those determined using modern GPS. Place names were written near places chosen on the maps to measure latitude. Errors or inconsistencies of a tenth to three-tenths of a degree could be as much the result of my own error in selecting the place on the map to measure as it could be an incorrect latitude indicated on the map. Nevertheless, if the latitudes indicated on the maps were the same or very close to those recorded in the *espejo*, it would allow the dating of some of the information contained in the *espejo* to be as early as 1526. The information would have been unchanged by the time it is thought to have been printed in the late 1520s or early 1530s.

The 1527 Colón map, enlarged and in black and white.
Measures 20" x 36"

The result of the research was the creation of a table indicating the latitude of selected toponyms as determined by GPS, the Chavez *espejo*, and the maps. The tables showed that the latitudes in the Chavez *espejo* were very close to those determined by modern GPS, and that the maps and the *espejo* were generally consistent.

Comparison of Latitudes

Colón 1527 Map—Latitudes

Place	GPS	*Espejo*	Map
Tropic of Cancer*	23.4	n/a	23.5
Santo Domingo (on Hispaniola)	18.4	18.5	18.0
Puerto Rico (San Juan) Port	18.4	18.5	18.0
Cabo de San Antón (Cuba)	21.7	21.5	21.5
Santiago (Cuba)	20.0	20.0	20.0
Río del Espiritu Santo (Miss. River)	30.0	30.0	28.0
Las Palmas (La Pesca, Mexico)	23.8	24.0	27.0

Río Pánuco (Tampico)	22.3	23.0	23.5
Veracruz (Villa Rica) Port	19.2	19.5	20.0
Bay of Juan Ponce (Tampa Bay)	27.5	27.3	27.5
Río de Canoas (Myakka?)	27.0	26.5	27.0
Río de la Paz (Peace River) C.H.	26.7	26.0	26.5
Tortugas	24.4	25.0	24.5
Martires (Keys) Midpoint	24.7	25.0	24.5

Ribero/Propaganda 1529—Latitudes

Place	GPS	*Espejo*	Map
Tropic of Cancer*	23.4	n/a	23.5
Santo Domingo (on Hispaniola)	18.4	18.5	18.0
Puerto Rico (San Juan) Port	18.4	18.5	18.0

Place	GPS	Espejo	Map
Cabo de San Antón (Cuba)	21.7	21.5	21.0
Santiago (Cuba)	20.0	20.0	n/a
Río del Espiritu Santo (Miss. River)	30.0	30.0	30.0
Río de Palmas (La Pesca, Mexico)	23.8	24.0	25.8
Río Pánuco (Tampico)	22.3	23.0	23.0
Veracruz (Villa Rica) Port	19.2	19.5	19,0
Bay of Juan Ponce (Tampa Bay)	27.5	27.3	26.5
Río de Canoas (Myakka?)	27.0	26.5	n/a
Río de la Paz (Peace River) C.H.	26.7	26.0	24.5
Tortugas	24.4	25.0	23.8
Martires (Keys) Midpoint	24.7	25.0	23.8

Ribero/Kohl 1529—Latitudes

Place	GPS	*Espejo*	Map
Tropic of Cancer*	23.4	n/a	23.5
Santo Domingo (on Hispaniola)	18.4	18.5	n/a
Puerto Rico (San Juan) Port	18.4	18.5	17.5
Cabo de San Antón (Cuba)	21.7	21.5	21.5
Santiago (Cuba)	20.0	20.0	20.0
Río del Espiritu Santo (Miss. River)	30.0	30.0	30.0
Río de Palmas (La Pesca, Mexico)	23.8	24.0	26.0
Río Pánuco (Tampico)	22.3	23.0	23.5
Veracruz (Villa Rica) Port	19.2	19.5	19.0
Bay of Juan Ponce (Tampa Bay)	27.5	27.3	26.8

Place	GPS	*Espejo*	Map
Río de Canoas (Myakka?)	27.0	26.5	26.0
Río de la Paz (Peace River) C.H.	26.7	26.0	25.8
Tortugas	24.4	25.0	24.0
Martires (Keys) Midpoint	24.7	25.0	24.5

* Modern technology places the Tropic of Cancer at 23.44°N in 2020 . (See Appendix II)

The latitudes on the maps generally complied closely with the latitudes indicated in the Chavez *espejo* and with GPS. The latitudes for toponyms on the west coast of Florida are remarkably accurate on the Colón map when compared with the *espejo* and GPS, as is the shape of Florida. The Ribero maps generally have Florida toponyms consistently about 1° off, to the south, and the Ribero maps are inaccurate as to the shape of Florida.

The only significant difference found between the maps and the *espejo* was the wildly inaccurate placement of *Río de Palmas* on all three maps, placing it from two to four degrees (140 to 280 miles) north of its position, as determined by the *espejo* and GPS. The *espejo* also describes a large and deep *Bahia Honda* on the west coast of Florida at 29°N, which is not indicated on the maps. No bay exists at 29°N on the west coast of Florida.

Major Findings of the Map and Latitude Study

The primary intent of the study had been to determine the location of the Bay of Juan Ponce and what Narváez knew about the coastal geography of the Gulf of Mexico before he left Spain. Only one toponym is labled as a bay on the entire Gulf Coast on the 1527 or 1529 maps, and it is the *Bahia de Juan Ponce*. Immediately south of the Bay of Juan Ponce is the *Rio de Canoas,* and further south of it is the *Rio de la Paz*, known today as the Peace River. The Peace River flows into present-day Charlotte Harbor. In every case, regardless of the latitude indicated for the Bay of Juan Ponce, the *Rio de la Paz* is shown to be at least one degree, or seventy miles, to its south.

Other maps would require examination to see if the mapped relationship of the Bay of Juan Ponce to the *Río de la Paz* would change in later years, or if any location south of the Bay of Juan Ponce was ever identified as a bay.

Early maps cannot be seen as the only evidence of the locations of bays, coastal anchorages, and routes of early inland explorations and settlements. They must be examined in the context of contemporaneous written descriptions found in chronicles, letters, and sailing directions of the same period. This requires a broader study than a simple examination of maps. To the information gained by a study of maps, other information must be added, especially relating to the knowledge that Ponce de León and Narváez had gained from personal experience in their more than twenty-five years in residence and travels in the Indies before their ill-fated final expeditions began.

CHAPTER SIX

Finding the Bay of Juan Ponce and the Likely Settlement Site

J UAN PONCE DE León established, or attempted to establish, the first European settlement in what is now the United States somewhere on the west coast of Florida in 1521. Since the year 2021 will mark the five hundredth anniversary of the event, it is an appropriate time to take a new look at what is known of Juan Ponce's expedition, particularly since large-scale contemporaneous maps displaying toponyms and latitudes are now available to augment previous research. For purposes of the orientation of key-named places on the west coast of Florida, a modern map has been provided, indicating current place names and their latitudes in order to compare these locations with maps described below (Map 18).

There have been conflicting conclusions drawn by historians as to where the settlement attempt was made, and whether or not a settlement was actually established. Some believe that when Juan Ponce arrived somewhere on Florida's west coast in 1521, he was immediately repulsed by the Indians. Others have concluded that a settlement was established and that it lasted three to four months. Whether or not the expedition succeeded in establishing a settlement, historians appear to agree that the settlement, or attempted settlement, was probably near Charlotte Harbor, the bay closest to where he is believed to have made a landing in his 1513 discovery expedition.

The Ribero and Colón maps add new evidence to the study as to whether or not a settlement occurred and where it may have taken place. While a few cartographers have noted that the Bay of Juan Ponce first appeared on these maps, none have provided details in their written descriptions as to where the Bay of Juan Ponce was located. With the exception of the USLC Colón map appearing in Adorno and Pautz, no enlargement of maps that show toponyms on the west coast of Florida c. 1527 appear to have been printed by previous historians or cartographers.

Ponce de León's First Expedition to Southwestern Florida in 1513

Juan Ponce de León is recognized to have been the "discoverer" of *La Florida* in 1513. Since the Spanish had first discovered the Bahamas twenty years earlier, he was surely not the first European to find or set foot on Florida. Independent operators, looking for gold and slaves, had surely found that "island" before.

Regardless of the date of discovery, Ponce de León had been granted the privilege by the king to officially "discover" and govern the island of Bimini and other lands that he might encounter in February of 1512, and he had discovered *La Florida* in 1513. Accounts of his exploration expedition were written many years later by Oviedo,[47] Bernal Díaz del Castillo,[48] Peter Martyr,[49] Bartolomé de Las Casas,[50] and

---

47   Gonzalo Fernández Oviedo y Valdés, *Historia General Y Natural De Las Indias: Islas Y Tierrafirme Del Mar Oceano.* Primary Source Edition. Madrid 1853. Published in U.S. in 1932. Reprinted by NABU Public Domain Reprints. (Obtained from University of Texas Library.) Undated.

48   Bernal Díaz del Castillo, *A True History of the Conquest of New Spain,* Hackett Publishing, 2012

49   Peter Martyr D'Anghiera, *De Orbo Novo.* Translated by F.A. MacNutt. Project Gutenberg, 2004

50   Bartolomé de Las Casas, *Historia de las Indias.* Translated by Andrew Collard, 1972

Antonio de Herrera de Tordesillas (Herrera).[51] The Herrera account, *Historia general de los hechos de los Castellellanos en las Islas tierra firme del Mar oceano,* is the most detailed and most cited, and is relied upon as the most complete primary source for information about the expedition. It was first published in 1601 in Madrid. The other accounts or references are so brief or obviously incorrect that, with the exception of a brief account by Oviedo, they have been generally discounted as being of any significant value in studies of the 1513 expedition.

Ponce de León had first discovered the east coast of Florida, then sailed around the southern end, and then north along the Florida west coast. His pilot was Antón de Alaminos, who had come to the Indies as a boy on Columbus's last voyage to the New World. There is no certainty as to how far north along the western Florida coast Juan Ponce explored. Herrera wrote that they had sailed north along the coast from the present-day Keys, then turned back south, arriving at an anchorage near an island, where they careened one of their ships. While many researchers appear to have accepted Pine Island as the presumed anchorage, others have written that it likely occurred

---

51   Worth, *Discovering Florida*, p.12

near Mound Key. There are numerous other islands in the area inhabited by the Calusa, and Juan Ponce's anchorage could have been near any of them.

Herrera's wording is important, as different inferences have been drawn from the Herrera account as to whether Ponce de León could have sailed as far north as Apalachee Bay or Tampa Bay. Herrera wrote:

On Sunday, the fifteenth of May, they ran along the coast of the Keys ten leagues down to two white keys. They gave the name los Martires to all this reef of islands and keys, because seen from a distance the rocks they project up seem to be men who are drowning, and the name also conformed to the many who have been lost on them afterward. They are at twenty-six degrees, fifteen minutes. They went navigating sometimes to the north, others to the northeast, until the twenty-third of May. On the twenty-fourth they ran along the coast toward the south (not realizing it was the mainland) down to some little islands that were located off the seashore. Because it seemed that there was an entrance between them and the coast for the ships to take on water and firewood, they remained there until the third of June, and careened a ship called the San Christobal.[52]

Herrera, a few paragraphs later, wrote, *"Friday, the fourth of June, while awaiting wind to go in search of Chief Carlos, whom the Indians on the ships said had gold, a canoe arrived at the vessels,"* indicating that his previous statement that they had remained *"until the third of June"* was at least one day off. (I believe that the name given by the chroniclers to the chief, "Carlos," may have been derived from Calusa).

It is possible to interpret Herrera as reporting that the ships had sailed north from the fifteenth of May until the twenty-fourth of May before they turned south, allowing nine days for their exploration to the north before they headed back south. It is also possible to interpret Herrera as stating that the ships sailed north on the fifteenth of May and reached their anchorage to the south on the twenty-fourth, leaving only nine days for the entire round trip along the Florida coast. I believe that a clear reading is that they sailed north from the fifteenth to the twenty-fourth, nine days, before heading back south to their

---

52   Worth, *Discovering Florida.* p. 51

anchorage site. This provided ample time for them to have gone as far north as Apalachee Bay, about 350 miles to the north, and/or Tampa Bay, which is 200 miles north of the Keys. Had they reached Apalachee Bay on the twenty-fourth before heading back south, they had nine days to reach an island south of today's Charlotte Harbor—about three hundred miles away— careen a ship, then depart on June 3. Had they only gone as far north as Tampa Bay, the total time of about sixteen to eighteen days from their departure from the Keys would have allowed them ample time to have sailed and explored the entire length of Tampa Bay.

Historians have long debated whether Ponce de León did, or did not, explore the coast as far as Tampa Bay or Apalachee Bay. T. Frederick Davis, apparently believing that only nine days had been available for the round trip, concluded that *"Had Ponce de Leon sailed continuously north from the Tortugas he would have sighted the coast at or near Tampa Bay. Had he taken a straight northeast direction, he would have come upon it in the vicinity of Cape Romano* [Cape Romano is just south of today's Marco Island, near Gullivan Bay]. *It follows then that under any circumstances, the actual contact was within these limits.*"[53] Harrisse argues that Ponce de León explored as far north as 30°, the latitude of Apalachee Bay.[54] His opinion is shared by Frederick Ober, who wrote that Ponce de León had "*sailed northward on the Gulf coast, probably to the bay of Apalachee.*"[55] Milanich, in "Charting Ponce de León's 1513 Voyage to Florida,"[56] wrote:

> *the three weeks Ponce spent within the Calusa Indian territory was sufficient time for one or more of his ships to explore the Gulf coast north of the present-day Lee County* [south of Charlotte Harbor] *area. That such a voyage took place is suggested by a notation on the 1519 map of the Gulf of Mexico coast (from Florida to the Yucatán) drawn as a result of the Alonso Álvarez de Pineda expedition. Written on the map at about modern*

---

53   T. Frederick Davis, "Juan Ponce de Leon's Voyages to Florida." The Quarterly of the Florida Historical Society. Volume XIV, Number 1. Tallahassee, Florida: Office of Publications, July, 1935. p.20

54   Harrisse, p. 153

55   Frederick Albion Ober, *Juan Ponce de León*, Harper Bros: 1904. p. 193

56   Viviana Díaz Balsera and Rachel A. May. *La Florida: 500 Years of Hispanic Presence.* Gainesville: University Press of Florida, 2014. Milanich, p.58

Apalachee Bay is 'Juan Ponce discovered to this point' (Map 2).

Since no better contemporaneous record than the Herrera account exists, how far north Ponce de León went, or whether he discovered Tampa Bay at that time, can't be determined with any degree of certainty.

What is known is that Juan Ponce sailed north along the Florida coast, then turned back, sailing south until he arrived at an island somewhere near the southern entrance to Charlotte Harbor in the area controlled by the Calusa. These islands all have one thing in common: the waters around and between them are extremely shallow, with average depths of five to eight feet, far too shallow for large ships to navigate.[57]

Soon after arriving, Juan Ponce careened (intentionally grounded, perhaps to repair a leak) one of his ships and sent men ashore who "bartered for skins and low gold."[58] The Ponce de León boats were later attacked

---

57   NOAA charts 11426 and 11427. Visible online at https://charts.noaa.gov

58   Antonio de Herrera y Tordesillas, *The General History of the Vast Continent and Islands of America, Commonly Call'd, the West-Indies, From the First Discovery Therof.* Translated by Capt. John Stevens. Vols I–III. London: Wood and Woodward. MDCCXL. Facsimile edition by Gale ECCO Print. Undated. p. 36

by Indians in twenty canoes, resulting in the deaths of four Indians and a Spaniard. In spite of the combat, and apparently more interested in finding gold than in taking a lesson from his discovery that the Indians were belligerent, Juan Ponce attempted to make peace with the Indians. Using a captured Indian who spoke Spanish, he arranged a meeting with their chief, Carlos, to arrange a peace.[59] The following day, Juan Ponce sent a bark to sound the harbor (another indication of the shallowness of the waters) and go ashore. When the Spanish arrived at the designated meeting place, they were attacked by a large number of Indians in canoes. Herrera wrote, "*And thus it was that at eleven o'clock eighty shielded [canoes] came upon the ship that was closest. They fought from morning until night, without injury to the Castilians, because the arrows did not reach them, since* [the Indians] *did not dare approach nearer because of the crossbows and artillery shots.*"[60] That was enough for Ponce de León, and he departed southern Florida to continue his search for "Binini." On his homebound voyage he discovered and named the *tortugas*, a group of small islands about seventy miles west of present-day Key West. He continued his

---

59   Davis, T. Frederick, p. 20

60   Worth, p. 6

search for Binini and stopped at an island where he encountered the pilot, Diego Miruelo, who had sailed there in a small bark from Hispaniola. Herrera wrote that Miruelo "was going exploring," although others say that he had arrived there by accident. Fuson had concluded that the island that they met on was Grand Bahama, and that Diego Miruelo had been dispatched by Velázquez to check on Juan Ponce.[61] Juan Ponce continued his exploration for Binini, finally arriving in San Juan at the end of September.

Juan Ponce de León from 1513-1521

There is no record of Juan Ponce having visited or sent any others to further explore *La Florida* between 1513 and 1521, perhaps because during that period he had spent considerable time in Spain. He had first returned to Spain in 1514 and was honored by King Ferdinand for his discovery with new titles and a renewed contract to settle *La Florida* on September 27, 1514.[62] He or his pilots would have been required to provide a full report with their recordings of latitudes, place names, and sailing routes to the pilot-major of the

---

61   Fuson, *Juan Ponce*, p. 112

62   Ober, p. 226

Casa de Contratación. It is likely that this information, and perhaps their maps, became available to others. This information was certainly known to the pilots and sailors of his expedition and was likely used for subsequent exploration of the Florida coast.

Juan Ponce had returned to his home in Puerto Rico in 1515. In January 1516 King Ferdinand died, and Carlos I ascended to the throne. Juan Ponce returned once again to Spain in 1516, this time to protect his rights and privileges, especially seeking to prevent Viceroy Diego Columbus from interfering with his claim to *La Florida*. He remained there until May of 1518.[63]

While Juan Ponce was in Puerto Rico or away in Spain, others had been visiting Florida. Harrisse wrote that "[Ponce de León] *had scarcely returned from his first voyage to Florida when other Spaniards followed in his path, and abducted Indians from the main land. Ponce appealed to the Crown for redress, his rights being thereby infringed, and in 1517, orders were sent to protect in his behalf los indios de Bimini.*"[64] Barcia wrote in his chronicles that in 1516 Diego Miruelo had gone from Cuba to Florida to barter with Indians for some gold,

---

63   Fuson, *Juan Ponce*, pp. 144–147
64   Harrisse, p.154

and having expended his trading goods, had returned directly to Cuba.[65] This is another reference to Diego Miruelo, the pilot who had been encountered by Juan Ponce on a Bahamian island during his 1513 discovery voyage, suggesting that Miruelo had found, by 1516, friendly Indians on the Florida coast. Based on Ponce de Leon's hostile engagement with the Calusa in 1513, it is highly unlikely that the Indians with whom Miruelo bartered were the Calusa. It is likely that Miruelo had found a tribe to trade with elsewhere, and this may have been the place that Juan Ponce would ultimately choose for settlement.

At least two unauthorized expeditions, other than Miruelo's 1516 bartering excursion, are known to have gone to Florida while Juan Ponce was in Spain. One was a slaving expedition sent in 1516 by Diego de Velázquez, the *adelantado* of Cuba, for which he had been reprimanded by the crown in the royal *cédula* of 1517.[66] Another was led by Francisco Hernández de Córdoba in 1517, who had gone to Mexico, battled Indians, and encountered bad weather. The main pilot

---

65   Andrés González de Barcia Carballido y Zúñiga, *Barcia's Chronological History of the Continent of Florida.* Translated by Anthony Kerrigan. Gainesville: University of Florida Press, 1951. Decade I, p.15

66   Fuson, Juan Ponce, p. 141

of his three-ship fleet was Antón de Alaminos, who had been on Ponce de León's discovery voyage to Florida. They sailed across the Gulf of Mexico and made landfall at the same place that Alaminos recognized he had been before on the 1513 voyage. The chronicler of the expedition, Bernal Díaz del Castillo, reported that it took four days to sail from the Yucatán to Florida. They were attacked by the Calusa and engaged in a fierce battle, during which one man was captured and never seen again. Many Indians were killed, and Spaniards were wounded.[67] Córdoba had already been badly wounded during their encounters with the Indians in Mexico. His men and ships retreated, running aground in the Martires (Keys) on the way, and barely made it back to Cuba. Córdoba died of his wounds ten days later.[68] Word of the combat between Córdoba's men and the Calusa would have become known to Juan Ponce, reinforcing his knowledge that the territory of the Calusa would be a risky place to attempt to establish a colony. It is likely that in making plans to establish a colony, Juan Ponce would have either sent an advance scout to find a good location or at least consulted with

---

67   Ober, p. 185

68   Fuson, *Juan Ponce*, pp. 143–144

captains and pilots that had visited *La Florida* since his last visit eight years earlier.

Juan Ponce's Decision to Establish a Settlement

In 1519, Camargo (Pineda) had made his voyage around the Gulf of Mexico and drawn a map, known as the Pineda map, showing *La Florida* to be connected by a landmass that extended to New Spain. Knowledge of this discovery, if not the map itself, probably became known to captains and pilots sailing the Indies some time in 1520, and thus to Ponce de León. Whether Ponce de León learned of this discovery prior to his decision to establish a settlement in Florida is unknown, but the timing of his settlement expedition suggests that he had learned that his own *La Florida* was connected to New Spain. In a letter to King Carlos on February 10, 1521, he wrote that he planned to return to *La Florida*, " . . . *taking a number of people to settle. I also intend to explore the coast of said island further, and see whether it connects with the land where Diego Velázquez is, or any other . . . I shall set out in five or six days.*"[69] His reference to the "land where Diego Velázquez is" refers

---

69   Robert S. Weddle, *Spanish Sea: The Gulf of Mexico in North American Discovery, 1500–1653.* College Station, Texas: Texas A&M University Press, 1985. p. 48

to the territory in Mexico where Cortés, thought to have been acting on Velázquez's behalf, had met with Camargo in 1519 and seen the Pineda map. Ponce de León had most likely heard a claim or seen a map that indicated that Florida was connected by land to what became known as New Spain. He also knew that Velázquez had sent an unauthorized excursion to explore the coast of Florida while he had been in Spain. This suggests that his letter to the king stating that he was leaving Puerto Rico to establish a settlement in Florida was intended to reinforce his claim to it, and that his small expedition may have been prepared in haste, as it was composed of only one hundred to two hundred settlers.

At the time that Juan Ponce set out to establish a colony in Florida, he had lived in the Indies for twenty-eight years, a number of them as the governor of Puerto Rico. During his years in the New World as a man of great wealth and high position, he would certainly have known many of the masters, captains, and pilots of ships. He was, in a word, "connected." While some historians have presented him as a man who sailed blindly to the coast of Florida, or as a man with virtually no idea of the coastal configuration or locations of bays along the coast, it is far more likely that the ship's captains and pilots, and Juan Ponce himself, had a very good idea as to where he would settle, and that his settlement would be welcomed, or at least tolerated, when he arrived. His expedition was clearly not composed of the many horsemen and soldiers that would be needed for an expedition of conquest, as he certainly knew would be the case if he returned to the lands of the Calusa that he had encountered in 1513.

The Route of the Settlement Expedition

Juan Ponce's settlement expedition left Puerto Rico on February 20, 1521.[70] He had personal experience sailing the southwestern coast of Florida in 1513 and certainly knew, at the very least, where the martires, the tortugas, and the island that he had visited were located. In addition to his own sailing records and maps, two maps had been drawn of the Gulf of Mexico area at the time he left Puerto Rico. They bear a closer look, as they both provide some geographical information about the coast of Florida that probably became known to local sailors. The first is the Pineda map (Map 2) of 1519. It shows two dots on the coast of Florida, likely representing Charlotte Harbor and Tampa Bay, indicating that these waterways were

---

70   Fuson, *Juan Ponce,* p. 163

known at the time. It also bears the legend in the area of Apalachee Bay, *Juan Ponce discovered to this point*, indicating that the pilots who drew the map believed that Ponce de León had been there in 1513. It appears likely that these pilots had seen the sailing records or maps that had been submitted to the *Casa de Contratación* when Juan Ponce had returned to Spain five years earlier. The Cortés map (Map 3) shows three waterways on the Florida coast, likely—ascending from south to north—Charlotte Harbor, Tampa Bay, and Apalachee Bay. Many dots, indicating barrier islands or shallows, are shown along the coast of Florida. Just north of the entrance to the bay at the mid-point of the Florida coast is a crescent-shaped island. This could be Anclote Key, also known as Anclote Anchorage, which is located thirty-five miles north of the entrance to Tampa Bay. (It was named, in various spelling iterations, as "Ancon Baya" on later maps.) From the Pineda and Cortés maps, we have learned that before, or contemporaneously with, Juan Ponce's 1521 settlement expedition, it was known that there were at least two waterways along Florida's coast. The southernmost one would certainly have been known to be the one that Ponce de León, and later Córdoba, had major battles with the Calusa.

Juan Ponce's planned destination is unknown, but

he likely would not have chosen the place that he knew was inhabited by hostile natives that had forcefully rejected his own attempt in 1513, and that of Córdoba in 1517, to establish friendly contact. His settlement expedition was described by Herrera as carrying two hundred men and fifty horses and *"mares and calves and pigs and sheep and goats and all manner of domestic animals,"* all of which came from his estates on Puerto Rico.[71] Robert Fuson disagreed as to the size of the expedition. Juan Ponce had written a letter to the Cardinal of Tortosa on February 10, 1521, that he would depart San Juan in five or six days with *"two ships and all the people that I can carry."*[72] Fuson wrote that two ships could not have accommodated more than one hundred people and ten horses. Even if only two ships had been employed, the carrying capacity of the ships would have depended on the size of the ships that they used. There is no description of the ships, only of the cargo they carried. If the ships were *naos*, they certainly could have carried the livestock and passengers described by Herrera, especially on a relatively short twelve-to-fourteen-day planned voyage from Puerto Rico to Florida. A settlement expedition

---

71   Worth, John E, p. 62
72   Worth, John E, p. 86

with only ten horses and one hundred settlers, as Fuson argues, would be very small, but it is possible that the proximity of the west coast of Florida to other islands with Spanish settlements may have been planned to become routine supply bases for more settlers, horses, livestock, and provisions after the first group had established a settlement. Whether one hundred or two hundred settlers were on the expedition, the numbers would hardly represent a force large enough to engage in combat with hostile natives who had swarmed the 1513 Ponce de León expedition with archers in canoes.

Duration of the Settlement

The dates that the Ponce de León settlement, or attempted settlement, occurred are not known, but it is known that he departed Puerto Rico in mid-February of 1521. It is also known that one of the ships, with the wounded and dying Ponce de León, reached Cuba in early July.[73] The other ship with a number of survivors reached Veracruz in mid-July. Hernán Cortés, in his third letter to the king, reported that *"News arrived from Vera Cruz that a ship had arrived belonging to Juan Ponce de León, who had been defeated on the*

---

73   Fuson, *Juan Ponce*, p. 172

mainland or island of Florida." Cortés had written his letter to the king as a chronological account of his siege of Tenochtitlán. The arrival date of the Ponce de León ship had occurred after July 11.[74]

Henry Harrisse had studied all available references at the time he published his 1892 masterpiece, *The Discovery of North America*, and determined that the Ponce de León expedition had left Puerto Rico on February 20, 1521 with two ships carrying men and horses. In early July, one of the ships with the dying Ponce de León had reached Cuba. The other ship had reached Mexico in mid-July. Harrisse concluded that it could not have taken five months for ships to have sailed from Puerto Rico to Florida, be rebuffed there before they could establish a landing place, and immediately departed. Allowing for a month or more at sea for the voyages from Puerto Rico to Florida and from Florida to Cuba and Mexico, the settlement in Florida would have lasted three to four months. Evidence that the settlement was not immediately repulsed is contained in both the Herrera and Oviedo chronicles. Oviedo noted that Juan Ponce's priests had attempted to Christianize the natives: "*the natives were fierce and warlike and ferocious, and but little disposed to hearken*

---

74   Padgen, p. 247 and endnotes 66 and 68 on p. 490.

to the monks and priests who had accompanied him to perform divine worship, as well as to advance the interest of the Church, although they preached much to them."[75] Herrera's account is a bit more detailed, describing the natives as savage and warlike and

> *not accustomed to quietude, or to the abandoning their liberty so easily upon the discretion or foreign will of other men, or upon the election of those friars and clerics who accompanied him* [Juan Ponce] *for the exercise of the divine cult and service of the church. Although they might preach as much as they wished, they could not be understood with the brevity that they or he who led them there had anticipated.*[76]

A landing attempt that had been immediately repulsed would not have enabled the friars and clerics to have "preached as much as they wished." Herrera's reference to the Indians' refusal to "abandon their liberty upon the discretion or foreign will of other men" also indicates that the Spaniards may have followed their usual practice of attempting enforced servitude on the

---

75   Harrisse, p. 157

76   Worth, p. 62

natives by force of arms. Harrisse wrote that *"historians are therefore mistaken when they represent the enterprise as having consisted in a traject, a disembarkment, a fight, and a prompt return home."* Fuson agreed with Harrisse's conclusions, writing, *"Juan Ponce was in Florida for at least four months before the disastrous battle with the Indians."*[77]

Modern technology can assist us with a re-examination of Harrisse's conclusions and establish the possible route of Ponce de Leon to Florida. Ponce de Leon had left Puerto Rico on or about February 20, 1521. We will use Tampa Bay as the place to measure approximate distances from, as it is nearly the exact midpoint on the west coast of Florida. According to sea-distances.org (established to provide modern mariners with distances and sailing routes from one port to another), the distance from San Juan, Puerto Rico to Tampa Bay, Florida is 1,200 nautical miles. At an average speed of four knots, the voyage would take twelve days. Cutting that estimate to an average speed of two knots would make the voyage twenty-four days. It is not known if Ponce de León stopped along the way, but it would have been unlikely unless weather or problems with one of his ships developed after they

77   Fuson, *Juan Ponce*, p. 166

left Puerto Rico. Juan Ponce had large estates on Puerto Rico and would have acquired his settlement supplies, horses, and livestock from his own estates and would have had no need to stop at another island on his way to Florida. To the contrary, a ship packed with seamen, settlers, livestock, and settlement supplies would have been anxious to arrive at their destination as soon as possible. The size of his ships is not known, but with horses, cattle, pigs, at least one hundred settlers, and at least thirty total crew, they would have been *naos* or large *caravelas*. If we assume a quick journey with no stops, he would have arrived in Florida in twelve to fourteen days. If we change the assumption to a very slow average of two nautical miles per hour and add a stopover of ten days that may have been necessitated by weather or to repair a ship, Juan Ponce would have reached the coast of Florida in thirty-four days. That would put his two ships on the west Florida coast no later than the end of March.

The next dates known to us are that Ponce de León was wounded in a battle with the Indians and had been taken by one of the ships to Havana, arriving in the first week of July. The other ship went to Mexico, arriving in mid-July. Relying once again on sea-distance.org, we know that the distance from Tampa Bay to Havana is 311 nautical miles and would take three days at a speed of four knots. Veracruz, Mexico is 927 nautical miles from Tampa Bay and would take nine days at four knots. Cutting their average speed in half, nearly to a standstill, would increase their sailing time to six and eighteen days, respectively. That would place their departure from the Florida coast on or near July 1. That leaves April, May, and June that cannot reasonably be accounted for as anything but a settlement. It is not credible that settlement ships crowded to their limit could have spent five months, continuously at sea, sailing from Puerto Rico to Florida and then to Mexico and Cuba. The inescapable conclusion is that Ponce de León had established a settlement and that it had lasted three to four months.

Previous Attempts to Identify the Bay of Juan Ponce

In the absence of the Ribero and Colón maps, historians have relied on written accounts. Virtually all of them have concluded that the Bay of Juan Ponce was located on the lower west coast of Florida, near Charlotte Harbor. This may have been due to a conflation of the sites of two different landings by Ponce de León on the west coast of Florida, the first in 1513 and the second in 1521, as he had similar experiences, battling Indians on both occasions. It appears that the Bay of Juan Ponce was thought to be the name of the place of his first landing near the main village of the hostile Calusa, whose chief was known as Carlos. The fact that Ponce de León had hostile encounters with native Indians on both of his landing expeditions has likely led to the conclusion by some historians that they both occurred at the same place.

T. Frederick Davis wrote in 1935 that:

> *it is proven that the only place visited by Ponce de León on the west coast was the Charlotte Harbor region"* [that has never been proven] and asked, *"is it reasonable to suppose that Juan Ponce, having a cargo a part of which required prompt landing, would spend time unnecessarily looking for another location? The direct evidence furnished by these records is not sufficient to permit a positive statement that Juan Ponce attempted to plant his colony at Charlotte Harbor, but it can be said that all inferences point that way.*[78]

The only "inference" he refers to is his own assumption that Juan Ponce would not have wasted time looking for a settlement place since he already knew of a place where he would be immediately met by

---

78   Davis, T. Frederick, p. 63

a large number of Indians that had violently rebuffed all previous attempts at landings by Europeans. A more reasonable inference is that Ponce de León would have chosen any place but the Charlotte Harbor area to establish a colony.

John Worth, writing seventy-nine years later, agreed with Davis:

> *Ponce de León led his ships back to the Southwest Florida coast, evidently landing at or close to their original landing site near the Calusahatchee River, and possibly very near the site of the 1517 skirmish (which Ponce's pilot, Antón de Alaminos, had recognized from the 1513 landings). This location was called the Bay of Juan Ponce by the cosmographer Alonso de Chavez no later than the mid 1530s.*[79]

The statement that "this location was called the Bay of Juan Ponce" by Chavez is not supported by the latitudes in the *espejo*. The *espejo* shows the Bay of Juan Ponce to be at 27 ¼° (the entrance to Tampa Bay is at 27.5°N), and it also includes latitudes and locations for the *Rio de Canoas* at 26 ⅔°N, (the latitude of the midpoint of

---

79   Worth, p. 19

the entrance to Charotte Harbor is 26.7°N), and below it, the *Río de la Paz* at 26°N. The *espejo* indicates the *Río de la Paz* to be 1 ¼°, or ninety miles, south of the *Bahia de Juan Ponce*.[80] Both the Ribero and Colón maps also show the *Río de la Paz* far south of the Bay of Juan Ponce.

Robert Weddle wrote in *Spanish Sea* that "*Official Spanish sailing instructions of 1583 place the Bahia de Juan Ponce in latitude 25°*," and that "*López de Velasco located the 'Bay of Carlos' near the keys and wrote that Ponce disembarked there and was fatally wounded.*"[81] Weddle was not the first to conflate the "Bay of Carlos" with the Bay of Juan Ponce. Today's San Carlos Bay is in the area that most researchers agree that Ponce de León made his 1513 landing. The conclusion that he was "fatally wounded" there is based on the incorrect assumption that the Bay of Carlos and the Bay of Juan Ponce were the same place. San Carlos Bay is located near present-day Sanibel, Pine, and Estero Islands and Estero Bay, where Mound Key (the site of a major Calusa town) is located. Shallow passes between these islands provide access into Estero Bay and into Charlotte Harbor and the three rivers entering it, the

---

80   Chavez, pp. 366–367
81   Weddle, p. 53

Caloosahatchee, Peace, and Myakka Rivers. John Lee Williams in *The Territory of Florida* also quoted Velasco as the "earliest source" to propose that the "*first Colony attempted on the North American continent was in the present San Carlos Bay area, although the exact spot is a matter of debate.*"[82]

Neither the Colón or Ribero maps, nor the *espejo*, were cited by Davis, Weddle, or Williams. Neither these maps nor the *espejo* have any reference to a "Carlos Bay." None of those who opined as to the landing place of Juan Ponce had referred to a map, nor had they referred to water depths in the area of San Carlos Bay. Settlement ships, whether caravelas or naos, could not have entered or sailed into Charlotte Harbor, Estero Bay, or between the islands leading to them. The water is simply too shallow.[83]

All those who had opined as to the landing site of Juan Ponce had relied solely on written sources, primarily on the accounts of Herrera and Oviedo. Both Weddle and Williams had cited Juan López de Velasco as an

---

82   Lindsey Wilger Williams, *Boldly Onward—A True History Mystery Related to the Incredible Adventures of America's "Adelantados" and Clues to Their Landing Places in Florida.* Charlotte Harbor, Florida: Precision Publishing, 1986. p. 51

83   See NOAA charts 11426 and 11427. Visible online at https://charts.noaa.gov; also Appendix III

additional source. Velasco did not become a senior chronicler of the Indies until 1567 and published his *Geography and universal description of the Indies* in 1574. Neither the account written by Velasco nor the sailing directions of 1583 were contemporaneous accounts and should not be seen as more reliable than the toponyms and latitudes that were indicated on the 1527 Colón and 1529 Ribero maps, and in the Chavez *espejo* of c. 1530, all of which locate the Bay of Juan Ponce by its latitude and by its proximity to the two rivers (not bays) south of it.

Of those historians who concluded that a settlement had occurred, Harrisse postulated that the expedition may have first attempted a landing near the Charlotte Harbor area and then moved north, "perhaps to Tampa or Wakasassee." (Wakasassee was the former name of a river just south of today's Cedar Key at 29.10°N). He added:

We may then suppose that this coasting led the Spaniards to the mainland on the north-west of the Florida peninsula, which Ponce de León had already visited . . . perhaps as far as the Bay of Juan Ponce, where it is not impossible that the great battle which resulted in his defeat was fought. This would explain in a measure the early presence of that designation, which is almost the only one to be found on the first cartographical delineations of Florida.[84]

Harrisse was referring to the Colón and Ribero maps, the first maps to name the Bay of Juan Ponce. He described both the 1527 and 1529 Ribero maps, pointing out that the Bay of Juan Ponce is shown, and wrote that the Bay of Juan Ponce is *almost the only* [designation] *to be found.*" He did not mention where the Bay of Juan Ponce was located or that among the other "designations found" were named rivers that were shown for the first time on a map. Nor did he note that the maps included latitude scales. His description is an excellent example of an instance where a cartographer can see the full map and read its toponyms, but the reader is only told about the things that the cartographer considers significant. He added *"for a complete description, we refer to the facsimile analysis given by Kohl,"* as if the reader could simply obtain the Kohl book and study the rare two-foot by three-foot maps.

Fuson wrote that Juan Ponce would have avoided the Charlotte Harbor area altogether. He explained that

---

84 Harrisse, p. 162

"Juan Ponce had a terrible experience with the Caloosa Indians during his first voyage to Florida, probably at Pine Island in Charlotte Harbor . . . it is highly unlikely that he would have chosen Pine Island or any of the other nearby islands—today's Sanibel, Captiva, Estero, or others—for the site of his Colony." He suggested that a location further north would have included good sites in Ft. Myers, Naples, Tampa Bay, and others. He added that *"On some maps drawn a century after Juan Ponce's second voyage, Tampa Bay is labeled 'the Bay of Juan Ponce.' This has caused a number of people to immediately jump to the conclusion that Juan Ponce's colony was somewhere on the shores of Tampa Bay. This label, however, is at best weak evidence for such a conclusion, and is probably not evidence at all."*[85] If Fuson had known that the Ribero and Colón maps were drawn, not a century after, but within six years after the Ponce de León settlement had occurred, he would undoubtedly have considered them to be better evidence.

Ponce de León knew that the waters around Charlotte Harbor were extremely shallow, as he had been there in 1513 and careened one of his ships near an island. The tidal range is four feet, from low to high tide. A

---

85   Fuson, *Juan Ponce*, p. 171

ship, even a shallow-draft brigantine, would have to be in very shallow water to make careening possible. Juan Ponce certainly would not have intended to establish a settlement on a small island. He would have sought a safe anchorage and a landing place on the mainland. It is very unlikely that his settlement ships, crowded with crews, settlers, horses, livestock, and settlement supplies, could have been anything other than *naos* or large *caravelas*. If he did have at least one *nao*, drawing ten to twelve feet, it would not have been able to sail into Charlotte Harbor, which has an average depth of twelve to thirteen feet. In the analysis of early sixteenth-century water depths surrounding the entrances to Charlotte Harbor, Professor Ping Wang noted that the areas around the entrances to passes into Charlotte Harbor would have been too shallow to traverse by ships drawing ten or more feet.[86] This is supported by Douglas Peck, who had sailed the route of Ponce de León. As noted previously, Peck had written, "*Charlotte Harbor has been proposed as the harbor they explored, but that location is a large, shallow, almost landlocked inland bay with only a tortuous, winding, dredged entrance through nearly three miles of offshore shoals. It hardly justifies the name harbor.*"

---

86   Wang, Appendix III

Peck thus confirmed that Charlotte Harbor would not have been suitable for navigation by large ships. The shallowness of the water, preventing settlement ships from reaching safe anchorages near the mainland, combined with the knowledge that the local Calusa were extremely hostile, would make it highly unlikely that Juan Ponce would have chosen that area for a settlement.

Ponce de León undoubtedly had an idea as to where he would establish a settlement, and he may have learned of a place with friendly Indians from the pilot, Miruelo. He knew Miruelo, whom he had encountered on a Bahamian island on his return from his 1513 discovery voyage. In 1516, Miruelo had gone to Florida to barter with the Indians: "*He bartered with the Indians for some gold. After expending the glass and steel baubles he carried to trade with the Indians, and without making further examination, he returned to Cuba.*"[87] Since Miruelo had found a place with friendly Indians, it was certainly not in Calusa territory. Could he have been trading with the Tocobaga, and could that information have become known to Juan Ponce? Was the place Miruelo had traded with the Indians Tampa Bay?

---

87   Barcia, *Chronicles*, Decade I, p. 156

The Colón and Ribero Maps Identify the Bay of Juan Ponce

The best evidence that Ponce de León actually established a settlement, and where it occurred, are the Ribero and Colón maps. Had Ponce de León attempted a landing at an unknown place and been immediately repulsed, there would have been no need to memorialize, on the official *Padrón General*, a "Bay of Juan Ponce." Alternatively, the naming of a known place where a settlement did occur and resulted in the death of the very famous Juan Ponce de León would have been worthy of recognition on an official map. The name *Bahia de Juan Ponce* is first seen on the Colón and Ribero maps, created six years after Ponce de León's death. Unfortunately, the cartographers who have studied these maps and described selected details contained on them failed to note that the 1527 and 1529 maps showed the Bay of Juan Ponce and other waterways on the west coast of Florida and also their latitudes and geographical relationships to each other. Since the maps themselves could not be provided in the books due to their scale, historians have had to rely on the descriptions made by the cartographers without seeing the details on the maps for themselves.

Today's Charlotte Harbor Was the *Río de la Paz*

A review of the Ribero and Colón maps and others drawn from reports of the later Hernando de Soto expedition confirms that no bay is shown south of the Bay of Juan Ponce. The *Río de Canoas* and/or the *Río de la Paz* (Peace River) are shown in every case to be well to its south. The Peace River flows into Charlotte Harbor and derives its name from *Río de la Paz*, the name originally given to today's Charlotte Harbor by the mapmakers of the *Casa de Contratación* sometime before 1527. The name endured for more than three hundred years. The name "Paz River," entering Charlotte Harbor, is shown on a United States Coastal Survey map of 1851 (Map 25), although other maps and written accounts had generally by that time anglicized the name to "Peace River."

It is likely that the *Río de la Paz* took its name from Ponce de León's earliest attempts to make peace with the Calusa and Chief Carlos, and that the *Río de Canoas* is the place that he and his men were led before being attacked by Indians in eighty canoes. Just to the north of today's Peace River, and also flowing into Charlotte Harbor, is the Myakka River, which is likely the river shown on maps of the early 1500s as the River of Canoes.

Both of the Ribero maps (Maps 19 and 20) and the Colón map (Map 21) identify the Bay of Juan Ponce.

The Propaganda map shows a *r. de la paz* to its south, while the Kohl shows a *r. de canoas*. The 1527 Colón map shows both the *r. de canoas* and the *r. de la paz* as located south of the *b: Juhanponce*. The latitude scales on the maps indicate that the *Río de la Paz* is from one to two degrees (70 to 140 miles) south of the Bay of Juan Ponce. The Chavez *espejo,* as noted earlier, located the *rio de la paz* one and a third degrees (about ninety miles) south of the Bay of Juan Ponce.

A comparison of toponyms shown on various maps from 1527 to 1570 are listed below, from north to south, beginning with Anclote Key, which lies just north of the entrance to Tampa Bay southward to the Martyrs (the Keys). Anclote Key is not shown on all maps.

The Ribero/Propaganda Map—1529* (Map 19)

- Acalaya (Anclote?)
- B. de Juan Ponce
- R. des para
- R. de la Paz
- Tortugas—Martires

The Ribero/Kohl Map—1529* (Map 20)

- Atalaya (Anclote?)
- B. de Juan Ponce

- R. de canoas
- Aguada
- Canico (Indian name for Florida)
- Tortugas—Martires

*Both maps were drawn in 1526 or earlier

The Colón Map—1527 (Map 21)

- Ancon baxo (Anclote?)
- B. de Juhanponce
- R. de canoas
- R. de lapaz
- R. Scapana*
- Tortugas—Martires

*The Colón map is the only map that indicates a *r. de scapana* as the southernmost river on the coast.

The following maps were first published long after the Ponce de León and Narváez expeditions. None are of the size or quality as those produced at the *Casa de Contratación*. There is no certainty as to the person who drew the maps or when they were originally drawn. It is on two maps, both believed to have been created from accounts of the survivors of the Hernando de Soto expedition, that a fictitious bay at 29°N, "Bahia

Honda," renamed on a later map as *"Bahia del Espiritu Santo,"* is first seen on maps.

The "Santa Cruz" Map—c. 1544 (Map 22)

The Alonso de Santa Cruz map is of an unknown date but is believed to have been drawn based on the explorations of the Hernando de Soto expedition and first published c. 1572. Its official title at the Library of Congress is *"Mapa del Golfo y costa de la Nueva España: desde el Río de Panuco hasta el cabo de Santa Elena . . . "* Original at the Archivo de las Indias, Seville.

- Anco[n]baxo.

- B. ho[n]da. This is the only map that has been found to identify a "Bahia Honda." It may have been drawn from the Alonso de Chavez *espejo,* in which the latitude of a nonexistent bay was indicated to be at 29°N latitude. Chavez had identified "Bahia Honda" to be at 29°N, but his *espejo* described Tampa Bay, as he wrote that its mouth was fifteen miles wide and it extended thirty miles inland.[88]

- Farallones (Cliffs)—There are no geologic cliffs on Florida's west coast. A possible explanation

---

88   Chavez. p. 366

that these were "scarps." A large sand dune that has eroded can leave "scarp" (a sand cliff) eight to ten feet high.[89]

- b. de Jua[n]po[n]ce
- R. decanoas
- R. Delapaz
- aguada
- tortugas—los martires

The Chavez "DeSoto" map—c. 1570 (Map 23)

This map is believed to have been drawn by Jerónimo de Chavez (the son of Alonso de Chavez), who was the pilot-major of the *Casa de Contratación* at the time. It is thought to have been produced c. 1570 and based on accounts of the survivors of the Hernando de Soto expedition. It was first published by Abraham Ortelius in *Theatrum Orbis Terrarum* in 1584.[90] The following toponyms are revealed:

- Baya de Sp[irit]o Santo (at the latitude shown on Santa Cruz map as Bahia Honda)

---

89   Al Hine. Professor Emeritus, University of South Florida College of Marine Science. Personal communication.

90   Library of Congress, loc.gov, "Ortelius Atlas."

- Juan de Ponce
- Río de Canoas
- Río de pas
- Aguada
- Tortugas—Martyres

On this map, the Bay of Juan Ponce is shown at 27.5°N, which is the GPS latitude of the entrance to Tampa Bay, and its depiction is quite accurate in that he shows it with an appendage to the north, next to the toponym *Juan de Ponce*.

Analysis of Toponyms

There is general consistency, from north to south, in most toponyms. In every case, the *Río de la Paz* is located south of the Bay of Juan Ponce. The insertion of a *Bahia Honda* at 29°N (identified as *Baya de Espiritu Santo* on a later map), where no bay or harbor exists, must be attributed to an error resulting from an incorrect latitude reported to the *Casa de Contratación*. With the exception of that aberration appearing only on much later maps, the locations of places are consistent.

Bahia Honda—This non-existent bay appears only on maps produced after the Colón and Ribero maps. The description of a large bay at 29°N is obviously the result of an incorrect latitude reported by a pilot returning to Seville, as there is nothing resembling a large bay at 29°N. It may have been caused by the simple mistaking of a "7" for a "9" on maps or sailing documents presented by returning pilots. Since *Bahia Honda* does not appear on the Colón or Ribero maps, the insertion in the *espejo* of a bay at 29°N had to have occurred after those maps were drawn. The *espejo* describes *Bahia Honda* (Deep Bay) and *Bahia de Juan Ponce* similarly.[91] Both are described as having three islands at their mouth, and both are large and clean. It appears that similar descriptions of Tampa Bay were made by different pilots, each reporting it to be at a different latitude. The *espejo* describes two bays, one at 27.3°N and another at 29°N, resulting in the creation of maps that complied with the *espejo*. *Bahia Honda* is described as being five leagues wide and ten leagues long, a description that can only fit Tampa Bay.[i]

Ancon Bayo (Anclote Anchorage)—Of special interest is a toponym variously written as *ancon basco, ancon bayo, atalaya, acalaya, ančobaxo,*

91   Chavez. p. 366

and anconbacco. On every map, it is shown just north of the Bay of Juan Ponce. Anclote Key (or island) by radiocarbon dating is known to have been there for more than one thousand years. It is just north of the Pinellas headlands, about thirty-five miles north of the entrance to Tampa Bay.

Bahia de Juan Ponce—Always shown south of "*ancon bayo*" (and its variations) and north of the River of Canoes. Kohl described the bays on Florida's west coast as seen on the 1527 and 1529 maps and concluded that the northern bay, at approximately 28°N, was the Bay of Juan Ponce.[92]

Río de Canoas—Always shown south of the *Bahia de Juan Ponce* and north of the *Rio de la Paz*.

Río de la Paz—It is always shown south of the *Río de Canoas*.

Aguada—Shown on various maps as "aguada" or "agnada," the toponym used by mapmakers to show where fresh water was available. *Aguada* is described in the Chaves *espejo* to be at 25 ⅔°. Aguada may have been the island today known as

---

92 See Appendix VI for more on Kohl and his analysis of selected toponyms.

Marco Island, which is located at 25.8°N, north of Cape Romano and Gullivan Bay.

R. Scapana—The toponym _r. scapana_ is shown only on the Colón map at the southern terminus of Florida. Kohl suggested that the name may have been meant to be _escapa_ (escape), and that this might indicate the place that the 1513 Ponce de León expedition, or the 1517 Córdoba expedition (visiting the same place that Ponce de León had in 1513), escaped from the Indians.[93] Jerald Milanich noted that on the 1514 Freducci map (Map 9) was a toponym, _Stababa_, which was the name for the major Calusa town located on Mound Key. He also cited a history by Hernando de Escalante Fontaneda, who was shipwrecked in 1545 and lived in that area for twenty years. In his written history, Fontaneda referred to the town as _Estantapaca_.[94] A recent documentary by archaeologist and filmmaker, Theresa Schober, _The Making of Escampaba: The Kingdom of Carlos_, identifies Mound Key in Estero Bay as the principal village of the Calusa, and the name of the entire

---

93　Kohl, p.145. Translated from the German in Appendix VI.
94　Balsera, _La Florida_, p. 59

territory of the Calusa as Escampaba. Since *r.*
Scapana is south of the *Río de la Paz* on the Colón
map, the determination of the origin of the name
is not critical to this study.

Canico—Appearing on the 1513 Argentinae map
as Coniello and on the Ribero maps as Canico. It
is believed by some to be a derivation of the Indian
name for Florida. Barcia, in his chronicles, wrote
that *Cautio* was the Indian name for Florida.[95]

The Transition of the Name *Río de la Paz* to Peace River

The *Río de la Paz* became known as the Peace River
sometime in the late eighteenth or early nineteenth
century, perhaps earlier. A map of Florida in Thomas
G. Bradford's 1835 *Comprehensive Atlas* indicates
the Peace River flowing into Charlotte Harbor (Map
24).[96] The names and locations of bays and rivers were
addressed by John Lee Williams in *The Territory of
Florida,* published in 1837.[97] Charlotte Bay, Carlos Bay,

---

95   Barcia, *Chronicles*, Decade I, p. 2

96   Thomas G Bradford, *Comprehensive Atlas—Geogaphical,
     Historical and Commercial.* Boston:1835

97   John Lee Williams, *The Territory of Florida*, 1837. pp. 24–25

the Macaco (Myakka) River, and the Peace River were described in detail:

> *From Boca Grande to Carlos Bay may be twenty-five miles. It has many islands, among which Pine is the largest. It has [sic] eight miles south of Bocca Grande. . . . Macaco River enters twenty-five miles east of Bocca Grande. Peace River also joins the Macaco near the entrance of the bay. . . . Talackchopko, or Peace River . . . rises in the interior from Lake Apopkochee, and pursues a westward course until parallel with Charlotte Bay; it then turns south for about eighteen miles and enters the north side of the bay, some miles below the mouth of Macaco River.*

The U.S. Coastal Survey map of 1851 identifies the Peace River as "Paz R," and shows it to be near the Myakka River, and north of the "Calousa-Hatchee" River, all entering Charlotte Harbor (Map 25). Another map of West Florida, in Morse's General Atlas of 1856, identifies a river entering "Charlotte Bay" as the "Tatakchooke or Pease Cr."[98] (Map 26)

Nothing in the Charlotte Harbor area was identified

---

98   Charles W. Morse. *Morse's General Atlas of the World*. New York: D. Appleton and Company, 1856.

as a bay on the Colón or Ribero maps, but as rivers. They are always indicated on maps as being well to the south of the Bay of Juan Ponce. Latitudes in the *espejo*, and as shown on maps, consistently place the *Río de la Paz* at least seventy miles south of the *Bahia de Juan Ponce*. The Bay of Juan Ponce is described in the *Espejo de Navegantes* by Chaves to be at a latitude of 27 ¼°N, fitting the GPS latitude of the mouth of Tampa Bay of 27.5°N. The later accounts by Williams in 1837 and the maps by Bache in 1851 confirm that the Peace River led into what had by then become known as "Charlotte Bay."

The Bay of Juan Ponce Was Most Likely Today's Old Tampa Bay

In the study of latitudes indicated on the Ribero and Colón maps, and in the *espejo*, the latitude of the Bay of Juan Ponce is consistently shown to be at least one degree of latitude (seventy miles) north of the *Río de la Paz*. Later maps also consistently locate the Bay of Juan Ponce north of the *Río de la Paz*. The c. 1544 Jerónimo de Chavez map (Map 23) has a latitude scale indicating the Bay of Juan Ponce to be at about 27.5°. (The entrance to Tampa Bay is at 27.5°N). His father's *espejo*, produced forty years earlier, locates the Bay of Juan Ponce at 27.3°N and the *Río de la Paz* to be at

26°, placing the Bay of Juan Ponce about 1½ degrees (one hundred miles) to its north. On all maps found, even those produced thirty to fifty years after the 1521 Ponce de León settlement, the Bay of Juan Ponce is shown well to the north of the *Río de la Paz*. Today's Charlotte Harbor was never identified by early Spanish mapmakers as a bay but as the *Río de la Paz*. The Bay of Juan Ponce was today's Tampa Bay.

The Bay of Juan Ponce can likely be more specifically determined to be the northwestern portion of Tampa Bay that is now known as Old Tampa Bay. The first subdivision of today's greater Tampa Bay into several distinctively named portions of the larger bay is found in the last chapter of the *Relación*, in the accounts from the Hernando de Soto expedition, and in maps and descriptions written in the late 1700s and early 1800s.

Cabeza de Vaca had returned to Spain in 1537 and met with King Carlos and Hernando de Soto, who had just been appointed the *adelantado* of *La Florida*. In the last chapter of his *Relación*, Cabeza de Vaca wrote that upon his return to Spain, he had met with those who had gone in search of his expedition, and they had ultimately found the entrance to the large bay reaching twelve leagues inland, about five leagues south of his original landing site. "*And five leagues below where we had disembarked, they found the port that entered seven or eight leagues inland, and it was the same one that we had discovered, where we found the crates from Castile . . . "* Since the crates from Castile were found near present-day Safety Harbor on Old Tampa Bay, this is the first indication that those who searched for Narváez had entered Tampa Bay proper and sailed its full length to the Tocobaga village where Narváez had found the boxes from Castile. Milanich wrote: *"That the Tocobaga [village] was located on Old Tampa Bay in the vicinity of the modern town of Safety Harbor is certain. Juan López de Velasco describes the location precisely."*[99]

Cabeza de Vaca described the huge bay that Miruelo and the others had found while searching for him, although he had not seen it himself. His description depended on reports from others whom he had met with after his return to Spain in 1537. *"This port is the best in the world, and it enters inland seven or eight leagues [21-24 miles]. And it is six fathoms [36 feet] deep at the entrance, and five near land . . . it lies one hundred leagues [300 miles] from Havana . . . in a line north to south with this town . . . and ships come and go from one place to the other in four days . . ."*

---

99   Milanich, *Florida Indians.* p. 73

Tampa Bay is 311 nautical miles from Havana.[100] It is also approximately thirty miles long, and the depth at the entrance, though not known with precision, was at least twenty feet in 1500. The description in the *Relación* as to the large bay's location relative to Havana complies with the location of the entrance to Tampa Bay. The depth of the water within it fits Tampa Bay and excludes Charlotte Harbor, which has an average depth of twelve to fourteen feet (two fathoms).[101]

The fact that Cabeza de Vaca related that he had learned, after his return to Spain, that ships routinely sailed from Havana to the large bay in four days indicates that the location of the huge bay was known in Spain at the time the *Relación* was presented to the king in 1537, and well before Soto left on his own expedition. Cabeza de Vaca's description of the huge bay surely induced Hernando de Soto to go to the place with "the best port in the world" to begin his inland expedition. No maps of the *Casa de Contratación* produced after 1527–1529, and before the Soto expedition of 1539, have been found, but Hernando de Soto would

---

100 Sea-distances.org

101 NOAA Chart 11426. Large scale of chart would make book-sized reproduction of details illegible. Visible online at https://charts.noaa.gov/PDFs/11426.pdf

certainly have seen an updated version of the Colón map, including new details provided by those who had "sailed from one place to the other in four days." Later accounts by Rodrigo Rangel would confirm that Soto expeditionaries knew that they had landed near the Bay of Juan Ponce and that it was a smaller bay, much further into Tampa Bay than the Soto landing site.

It is widely accepted that Hernando de Soto, in his expedition of 1539, first made landfall in shallow waters just south of the entrance to Tampa Bay. Longboats and brigantines led the deeper-draft vessels to an anchorage inside Tampa Bay, near the mouth of present-day Little Manatee River.[102] The identification of the Bay of Juan Ponce (Old Tampa Bay) as being separate and distinct from what we now call Tampa Bay is first related by the *Relación* of Rodrigo Rangel in his account of the Hernando de Soto expedition. Rodrigo Rangel was the private secretary of Hernando de Soto and kept a diary of the entire expedition. Although the diary has been lost, Rangel was required to give a full account of the expedition to Gonzalo Fernández Oviedo y Valdés (Oviedo), who was the official chronicler of the Indies at the time. The Rangel account is generally considered to be the most accurate of the four major extant accounts

---

102 Milanich, *Florida Indians*, p. 129

of the De Soto expedition. Oviedo had written, "*The land where they disembarked is due north of the island of Tortuga . . . and it is ten leagues west of the bay of Juan Ponce.*"[103] That is a very telling description. Tampa Bay is located due north of the Dry Tortugas. "Ten leagues west" of a coastal bay would normally put one far out to sea. Only at the entrance to Tampa Bay could one be approximately thirty miles west (actually southwest) of another bay. The approximate site of the Soto landing is thirty miles southwest of Old Tampa Bay (Map 27). The fact that Rangel knew his proximity to the Bay of Juan Ponce confirms that after the Colón map was drawn to indicate the Bay of Juan Ponce to be a single large bay, it was later recognized to be a "bay within a bay," much further into Tampa Bay from the place that Soto had landed.

The evidence from early Spanish maps and chronicles supports the conclusion that the Bay of Juan Ponce is the area of greater Tampa Bay that is today known as Old Tampa Bay. Cabeza de Vaca's *Relación* states that the ships that had gone searching for Narváez had ultimately found "the best harbor in the world" and that

---

103 Clayton, Lawrence A., Vernon James Knight, Jr., and Edward C. Moore. *The DeSoto Chronicles* Univ. of Alabama Press, 1993. "Introduction—Rangels's Account of the Expedition" by John E Worth. Vol. I, pp. 249–254

it was the same place that Narváez had found "many boxes from Castile." The Rangel account indicates that those on the Hernando de Soto expedition knew that the Bay of Juan Ponce was located thirty miles east of their landing site near the entrance to Tampa Bay and had named the larger bay *Bahia del Espiritu Santo*. The Chavez "De Soto" map (Map 23) shows a northwestern appendage to the bay with *Juan de Ponce* written near that appendage. The conclusion drawn from the Colón and Ribero maps and the Chavez *espejo* is that the Bay of Juan Ponce was the name originally given by the Spanish mapmakers to all of today's Tampa Bay. The Soto expeditionaries named the main bay *Bahia del Espiritu Santo*, recognizing that the *Bahia de Juan Ponce* was an appendage thirty miles to the east, in essence a small bay extending from a larger bay.

That today's Old Tampa Bay became, in modern times, known by its present name, and distinct from the larger bay, likely first appears on a map by William Stork in 1767, drawn four years after the British took possession of Florida (Map 28). Stork identified the main bay as Spirito Santo Bay and the appendix north and west of the entrance as "Bay of Tampa." (Note that this map also shows "Carlos Bay" to be south of Spirito Santo Bay.) He prepared the map for the Earl of

Hillsborough, who was Secretary of State for the British Colonies at the time. Mapmakers after that attached the name Hillsborough to both the northeastern part of the bay and the river nearby.[104] The George-Louis Le Rouge map c. 1773 was headed Baye de Spiritu Santo. A small portion of it was named Hillsborough Baye, and the small appendage to the north, Tampa Baye (Map 29).

One bay, originally mapped by the *Casa de Contratación* in 1527 and 1529 as the *Bahia de Juan Ponce*, had become three bays in the ensuing 250 years. The Soto expedition had recognized it as two bays: the larger they named *Bahia del Espiritu Santo,* and the smaller one remained the *Bahia de Juan Ponce*. After the British acquired Florida, it became three bays, the Bay of Spirito Santo, Tampa Bay, and Hillsborough Bay. When the U.S. acquired Florida from Spain in 1821, the name *Bahia del Spiritu Santo* was dropped, the small bay to the northeast remained Hillsborough Bay, and the larger bay took the Tampa name for itself, relegating the original Tampa Bay to "Old Tampa Bay."

---

104 Arthur R. Savage and Rodney Kite-Powell, *Tampa Bay's Waterfront: Its History and Development.* Art. R. Savage & Son: Tampa, 2016

The location of a separately named bay is also described by Williams in 1837:

Tampa Bay, called by the Spanish Espiritu Santo, is the largest bay in the Gulf of Mexico. It is between 27° 4' and 28° N. latitude. . . . It is forty miles long, and in one place thirty-five wide, and has from eighteen to twenty feet of water on the bar. . . . The eastern part of the bay was by the British called Hillsborough, and the little bay attached to the north side, Tampa. The little Tampa is an elliptical basin about ten miles in diameter, but very shoal.[105]

This description of "little Tampa" fits what is now known as "Old Tampa Bay."

An analysis of the water depths of Old Tampa Bay indicates that *naos* of a size and draft (ten to twelve feet) suitable for a settlement expedition could have entered and anchored in Old Tampa Bay, and *caravelas*, drawing seven to eight feet, would have been able to easily enter and navigate the bay. A current NOAA (National Oceanic and Atmospheric Administration) chart of Old Tampa Bay shows depths of twelve to sixteen feet in many places at

---

105 Williams, John Lee, p. 24

mean low water (MLW), the lowest of the two daily tides, averaged over ten to fifteen years.[106] Old Tampa Bay has been subjected to a significant amount of human engineering in the last century, particularly the construction of causeways. Earlier bathymetric data was employed to determine the depth of the bay, and the pass into it, before human engineering. The tidal prism of Old Tampa Bay would have created a wide and deep main channel into Old Tampa Bay of approximately twenty feet in depth.[107] Estimating the depth within the bay in the early sixteenth century can be accomplished by using current bathymetric data and then adjusting for the sedimentation rate during the past five hundred years. According to a personal communication from Professor Gregg Brooks of the Eckerd College Department of Marine Science, the current average depth of Old Tampa Bay ranges from ten to thirteen feet at mean low water (low tide). The 500-year sedimentation rate estimates a range from a low of 10 to 30 centimeters (4 to 12 inches) based on Carbon-14 dating to 1.7 to 3 meters

---

106 NOAA Chart 11426. Large scale of chart would make book-sized reproduction of details illegible. Visible online at https://charts.noaa.gov/PDFs/11426.pdf

107 Wang, Appendix III

(5 to 9 feet) based on Pb-10 radiocarbon dating. The lowest sedimentation rate assumption indicates that Old Tampa Bay would have been four to twelve inches deeper in 1500, providing an average depth in Old Tampa Bay, at low tide, ranging from eleven to fourteen feet five hundred years ago. High tide would add approximately three feet over MLW, bringing the depth to fourteen to sixteen feet twice a day. While there were certainly shallows within the bay that might have caused larger ships to ground at low tide, this would not have been unusual. The fact they may have is suggested by Cabeza de Vaca, who described the "best harbor in the world," adding that "its bottom is of soft, fine sand," something sailors could not have known if they had not had occasion for their ships to settle at low tide. There is no doubt that ships drawing ten to twelve feet could have entered and anchored within Old Tampa Bay in the early sixteenth century.

To all of the above must be added a common-sense analysis of the expedition of Juan Ponce de León. He had set out to establish a permanent settlement from which he would "*explore the coast of said island further, and see whether it connects with the land where Diego Velázquez is, or any other,*" as he had written to the king in February 1521. A location near the southern tip of Florida would significantly increase the distance he would have to travel to make such a northward and westward exploration. Juan Ponce knew that the Calusa and their chief, Carlos, were extremely hostile and treacherous. He had twice, in 1513, had deadly encounters with the Calusa. He surely also knew of the disastrous encounter that Córdoba had with the Calusa in 1517. Juan Ponce would have known that it would be virtual suicide to attempt a settlement in the lands of the Calusa, especially with only one hundred to two hundred people. He also knew that the waters in the area he had previously visited were extremely shallow, presenting a significant risk of the grounding of his heavily laden ships.

The largest bay on the west coast of Florida would have been known to Juan Ponce or his pilots. Numerous ships had traveled to the west coast of Florida before and after the Pineda expedition of 1519. It is likely that information concerning the west coast of Florida was gained from Diego Miruelo, or from sailors who had accompanied him, on his 1516 trading mission to the west coast of Florida. Whether or not Juan Ponce had previously discovered Tampa Bay on his 1513 expedition, he and his pilots would surely have known that there was a large bay north of the area controlled by the Calusa. The northern shore of the large bay was in the lands of the Tocobaga, enemies of the Calusa, who may have been considerably less hostile to European visitors.[108]

Juan Ponce's route to Florida would have been from Puerto Rico, past Hispaniola and Cuba. He would not have gone ashore in Cuba, as Velázquez, the governor of Cuba, had already infringed on Ponce de León's territorial rights by sending an expedition to Florida. Juan Ponce's complaints had led to an official censure of Velázquez by the king. Juan Ponce would not have seen Cuba as a destination worth a visit as he headed toward his own dominions in *La Florida*.

Juan Ponce would have reached the Tortugas (he had discovered them in 1513) before heading north to the coast of Florida. While maps identifying the *martires* are generally believed to represent today's Keys, it is likely that the *martires* drawn on maps were intended to represent navigational barriers from the present-day Keys, much further to the west. West of Key West is a line of islands, known today as the Marquesas, and then numerous reefs. Ponce de Leon and his pilots likely knew that attempting to find a gap between the *martires* and the Tortugas would be risky and that staying west of the Dry Tortugas, "leaving them to

---

108 Fernando   Santos-Granero.   *Vital   Enemies.*   Austin: University of Texas Press, 2009. p. 86

starboard," would be the safest and surest way to avoid reefs and shoals before heading north or northeast to the mainland.

Once reaching the huge Tampa Bay, Juan Ponce's ships would seek a protected anchorage. Tampa Bay is seven to twelve miles wide, deep enough for large ships, and extends inland for thirty miles. Since he was looking for lands to settle, fresh water, and grass and vegetation for his livestock, he would have sailed inland, away from the heavy seas and storms of the Gulf, and away from the beaches and sandy soil. A near-perfect anchorage and settlement site would be in today's Old Tampa Bay. Old Tampa Bay's 360° circumference (Map 33) is entirely protected from heavy seas coming from the Gulf to the west . . . a perfect anchorage.

Seven years later, Pánfilo de Narváez would make an inland expedition from his landing site on the Pinellas coast to Tocobaga on the shores of Old Tampa Bay. He would unknowingly discover the site of the first colony established by Europeans in what is today the United States.

CHAPTER SEVEN

Revisiting the 1527 Pánfilo de Narváez Settlement Expedition

U PON HIS APPOINTMENT in December 1526 as the new *adelantado* of the lands that were formerly the provinces of Garay and Ponce de León, Narváez began to assemble his fleet and expedition settlers and forces. He would need to acquire ships, pilots, sailors, soldiers, settlers, settlement supplies, maps, and sailing directions. He would spend the next six months buying the ships and supplies he needed and hiring those who would join him to claim his vast new territory. Seville was a very busy place in the first six months of 1527. Fifty-nine ships had left Seville in 1526, bound for the Indies. In 1527, Narváez's five ships would represent only a small portion of the sixty-eight ships that sailed to the New World that year.[109]

---

109 Haring, p. 339

Joining Governor Narváez as an officer on the expedition was Álvar Núñez Cabeza de Vaca, who had been appointed as the expedition's treasurer by the king. Other members of the expedition included Captain Alonso del Castillo Maldonado, Andrés Dorantes de Carranza, and the slave and personal manservant of Dorantes, Estevanico. They would become, with Cabeza de Vaca, the only ones to survive Narváez's three-hundred-man inland expedition in *La Florida*.

Narváez was no stranger to Mexico, Cuba, and the other islands in the growing Spanish empire in the Indies. He had first sailed to Hispaniola sometime between 1493 and 1499. He had been a leader in the conquests of Jamaica in 1509, and Cuba in 1512–1514. He had lived in Cuba (when not in Spain or in prison in Mexico) since 1514. He certainly knew the island of Cuba well. He had become a rich man with numerous large estates, a high position, and many contacts on the island. He also had a lot of experience at sea. He had sailed from Spain to the Indies in 1499 or earlier, back to Spain in 1515, back to Cuba in 1519, back to Spain in 1525, and was now embarking on his third trip to the Indies. He also knew the Caribbean and Gulf well. He had sailed from Cuba to Veracruz on his ill-fated expedition to capture Cortés in 1520 and had sailed from Mexico back to Cuba in 1524 when he was released from prison by Cortés. He knew the locations of Cuba, Hispaniola, Puerto Rico and Jamaica, and their positions relative to each other and to Mexico and Florida.

In preparing for departure from Spain, Narváez and his pilots were required to complete the necessary documents confirming their authorization for the expedition. This was done at the *Casa de Contratación* in Seville, located about fifty-five miles up the Guadalquivir River from the seaport of Sanlúcar de Barrameda. Seville was the site of the Alcázar (Moorish word for castle) of Seville. It had been the castle of King Ferdinand, and much of it had been taken over by the *Casa de Contratación*. Seville was a major city and the primary source of ships, provisions for the voyage, pilots, soldiers, and seamen to man the ships. Ships of the early sixteenth century sailing to the New World were usually the *nao*, averaging in size from 100 to 200 *toneladas*, which meant that they could carry from 150,000 to 300,000 pounds of cargo.[110] Smaller caravels often accompanied the fleets as advance scouts, as their shallower draft allowed them to lead the way for the larger ships when nearing land or shallows. A royal *cédula* of 1522 had established the minimum

---

110 Perez-Mallaina, *Spain's Men of the Sea*, p. 66

requirements of the size of the crews and armaments that must be carried by ships sailing to the Indies. Every ship of one hundred to two hundred *toneladas* was required to carry a crew of thirty, including at least eighteen mariners, two gunners, eight apprentices, and two "ship's boys" (pages, usually aged eight to ten). Required armament consisted of at least eight cannons and a specified number of arquebuses, crossbows, pikes, lances, and sufficient powder and molds to make ammunition.[111]

Since ships sailing for forty to sixty days through many nights and foggy or stormy weather could easily be separated, it was important that each ship could operate and find its destination independently. There was a chief pilot, but each ship had to have at least one competent and informed pilot of its own. The pilot had the skill to get the ship thousands of miles across an open sea to an intended destination. Establishing location with complex instruments and calculations required teamwork. No pilot could work twenty-four hours a day. There would have been two pilots on each ship, or perhaps one who was assisted by apprentices or seamen who were working their way up toward becoming pilots themselves.

---

111 Roger Smith, p. 158

In his petition to the king, Narváez had made specific requests and promises as to his "subjugation of the countries there from the Río de Palmas to Florida." With the approval of the king came several changes to his petition. Across the last three paragraphs of his petition was written the requirement, "he must populate."[112]

When Narváez and his pilots met with cosmographers and pilots at the *Casa de Contratación*, it had been six years since the Ponce de León settlement survivors had returned from the west coast of Florida in 1521. There had also been countless trips by other vessels from islands in the Caribbean to various areas around the Gulf coast, very likely to Florida, which lies only about one hundred miles north of Havana. There had been numerous trips from Cortés's ships to Cuba and then back to Veracruz from 1521 to 1527. The sailing directions between the islands of the Indies, and from the islands to Mexico, would have been well-known by the pilots of the day. The presence of the islands of the Dry Tortugas, about 120 miles north/northwest of Havana, were also known and used for landmarks for sailing directions, as they had first been discovered by Ponce de León in 1513. All of this information would

112 Buckingham Smith, p. 210

have been duly recorded and used to update maps and the *espejo* maintained at the *Casa de Contratación*.

The *Casa de Contratación* would have provided Narváez and his pilots with specific information concerning the territory that he had just been appointed to conquer and govern. It appears that the Colón map was produced especially for him. It contained a number of changes from the earlier Cortés and Ribero maps. The 1520 Cortés map (Map 3) had indicated a "*Río della Palma*" far south of Pánuco near the Yucatán, and another river, "*Río, la palma*," north of Panuco. The later Ribero maps had added the heading, "*Tiera de Garay*," added the Bay of Juan Ponce, and changed the names of two of the rivers on the Cortés map. The result was that the Ribero maps have two rivers with identical names: a "*R de palmas*" to the north of Pánuco and another "*R de palmas*" far south of Pánuco near the Yucatán (Maps 30 and 31). The Colón map (Map 32) changed the heading on the Ribero maps from *Tiera de Garay* to *Tierra que aora va a poblar panfilo de narbaez* and had also changed the names given to the identically named rivers. In light of the need to avoid another territorial dispute between Narváez and Cortés, there was an obvious need to establish a place-name for the river marking the southernmost boundary of the Narváez territory that could not be confused with a river of an identical name within the territory of New Spain. The name of the southernmost river was slightly changed on the Colón map to r. *de las palmas*, in black ink, and the northern one was labeled as *las Palmas*, in red ink. The Colón map had another subtle change. Where the Ribero maps had indicated a *R. de montañas* (River of Mountains), the Colón map had changed it to *montañas* (mountains), just south of *las Palmas*. The identification of mountains was likely intended to provide a navigational landmark to Narváez's pilots. The river then known as *Rio las Palmas* is generally believed to be the present-day Río Soto la Marina, near La Pesca, about 160 miles north of Tampico (Pánuco).[113] Just south of the Río Soto la Marina are mountains that would be visible from offshore.

Narváez would certainly have obtained maps and latitudes of key ports along the entire coastline of his domain, from *Las Palmas* to the Cape of Florida, and especially that of his primary destination. The latitudes for *Las Palmas* on the Colón map and for the *Río de Palmas* on the Ribero maps are grossly incorrect, with all of them showing it at 25.8° to 27°N. The actual latitude of the river widely believed to be the *Río de las*

---

113 Reinhartz and Saxon, p. 114

Palmas (Río Soto de Marina) is at 23.8°N by GPS, and the *espejo* shows it at 24°N. The difference in distance between the actual latitude and that shown on the maps is 140 to 210 miles. Such huge errors in latitudes do not appear elsewhere on the maps. Had Narváez sailed to the latitude indicated on the Cólon map, he would have arrived near today's Corpus Christi Bay, at 27.5°N. Since Narváez actually never arrived anywhere on the east coast of Mexico, we will leave it to future researchers to attempt to reconcile that anomaly.

Narváez had at least five captains and five pilots when he left Spain. At least one person on each ship was required to have official maps and the latest *espejo* with them when they left Spain. From the array of maps known to have been available at the *Casa de Contratación*, and from their personal experience in the Indies, it becomes obvious that Narváez and his pilots knew the shape of the Gulf of Mexico, the geographic relationships of Cuba, Mexico, and Florida to each other, and general locations of ports and rivers along the Gulf coast. They certainly knew that Florida was on the east side of the Gulf, and Mexico on the west. Pilots would have carried their maps and navigational instruments with them when they went ashore in order to establish a stable platform from which to precisely determine their latitude.

Maps were only useful once land had been spotted. The fleet had to first get to the Indies. Narváez would follow the "*Carrera de Indias*" (Route to the Indies). The first stop after a seven-to-ten-day sail southwest from Sanlúcar de Barrameda would be at the Canary Islands, where they would have a brief respite while adding water and firewood for cooking, and perhaps some other provisions and men.

At the time he left Spain in 1527, Narváez was a forty-nine-year-old seasoned veteran with many years of commands and conquests behind him. Cabeza de Vaca was thirty-seven, while Dorantes, Castillo, and Estevanico are believed to have been about twenty-seven years old. None but Narváez had ever been to the Indies before. Narváez had significant experience in the Indies, having been there for more than twenty-five years. Narváez knew the island of Cuba, the ports there, and the directions from Cuba to the Mexican coast and to *La Florida*. Since it was his own idea to define his territory as all of the lands from the River of Palms to the Cape of Florida (combining the former provinces of Garay and Ponce de León), he would certainly have known what the boundaries of his territories were and obtained maps and information about the area that he was entitled to govern. He was acutely aware, based on his own unfortunate experience in the Velázquez/Cortés debacle in Mexico, of the consequences of a failure to firmly establish territorial boundaries authorized directly by the king. He would have been certain, before he left, that the officials at the *Casa de Contratación* were fully aware of the extent of the lands that he was entitled to settle and govern. The words inscribed across his petition when it was approved by the king, that "he must populate," had likely led to the wording on the Colón map, "the land that Pánfilo de Narváez is now going to populate."

On June 17, 1527, Narváez, with a fleet of five ships and six hundred men, set out from Spain, heading for the Indies four thousand miles away. His fleet arrived at Santo Domingo on the island of Hispaniola in late July or early August 1527. He spent forty-five days attempting to obtain horses and provisions for the settlement expedition, during which time more than 140 of his men deserted. Narváez acquired another ship in Hispaniola and his fleet of six ships sailed in mid-September for the port of Santiago, a large port on the southern coast of Cuba, closest to Hispaniola. It had been the home of Narváez's mentor, Velázquez, who had died in 1524. It was also the closest port to San Salvador de Bayamo, about seventy miles inland to the northwest, where Narváez had been appointed its *regidor perpetuo* (councilor) by King Carlos in 1518.[114] He certainly would have paid a visit to his estate and to his all-enduring wife, Maria de Valenzuela. Narváez obtained men, arms, and horses in Santiago. He had a contact in Santiago who said that he could supply more provisions at the port of Trinidad (not to be confused with an island of the same name), which was about three hundred miles to the west on the southern coast of Cuba. The entire fleet of six ships left for Trinidad but stopped halfway there at the port of Cabo de Santa Cruz. Narváez sent Cabeza de Vaca with two ships to pick up the provisions in Trinidad. Cabeza de Vaca arrived at the tiny port and was immediately advised to depart as soon as possible because it was an unsafe anchorage and many ships had been lost there. The following morning, he went ashore to obtain the provisions that were waiting for him, leaving most of his men aboard the ships. While Cabeza de Vaca was ashore, a hurricane hit, sinking the two ships. Sixty men and twenty horses were lost. Only thirty men of his original complement of ninety were left alive. Narváez had experienced the same hurricane but had been in the safer port of Cabo de Santa Cruz. He sailed to the devastated port of Trinidad with his

---

114 Adorno and Pautz, Vol. I, p. 377

four ships and ordered Cabeza de Vaca to take the ships to Jagua (modern-day Cienfuegos), as it was a much larger and better-protected port. Narváez had decided that Cabeza de Vaca and the four ships would spend the winter there. It is likely that the captains and pilots of the four ships met during the ensuing three to four months with their counterparts from other ships, updating their maps and charts with the latest knowledge concerning harbors and sailing directions. It is traditional for sailors to seek "local knowledge" from other sailors. While maps at the *Casa de Contratación* had been updated to the time Narváez had left Spain in June 1527, the opportunity during the winter of 1527 for pilots and sailors to compare and update notes and maps from other pilots wintering in, or passing through, Jagua should not be overlooked. Sailors depend on other sailors to advise them of landmarks, navigational barriers, and the locations and latitudes in order to confirm the thoroughness and accuracy of their own maps and sailing directions. Narváez would have spent the next three months at his estate with his wife and traveling the island to other towns and ports seeking more ships, men, and supplies.

In February, Narváez arrived in Jagua with a brigantine that he had purchased in Trinidad, accompanied by a pilot named Miruelo who had knowledge of the Gulf coast and the *Río de las Palmas*. Although the *Relación* and the Joint Report do not provide a first name for the pilot that accompanied Narváez, it is likely that Diego Miruelo is the pilot who joined the Narváez expedition in Cuba. There is evidence in both Herrera's and Barcia's chronicles that a pilot named Diego Miruelo knew the coast of Florida and where Cuba was in relation to it. Herrera wrote that on Ponce de Leon's discovery voyage in 1513, Juan Ponce had landed at an island in the Bahamas and met *"Diego Miruelo, the pilot, whom they encountered with a bark from Hispaniola, and who was going exploring, although others say that he arrived there by accident."*[115] Barcia wrote in his *Chronicles* that in 1516 *"Diego Miruelo, pilot, sailed from Cuba, setting a direct course for Florida. He bartered with the Indians for some gold. After expending the glass and steel baubles he carried to trade with the Indians, and without making further examination, he returned to Cuba."*[116] Buckingham Smith wrote that the Diego Miruelo of the Narváez expedition was the nephew of

---

115 Worth, John E., p. 53

116 Barcia Carballido y Zúñiga, Andrés González de. *Barcia's Chronological History of the Continent of Florida*. Translated by Anthony Kerrigan. Gainesville: University of Florida Press, 1951. First Decade. P.3

the elder Diego, who had been a pilot on the Pineda and Garay expeditions and had died during the Ayllón expedition of 1526.[117] If so, the younger Diego would very likely have sailed with his uncle as he learned the trade and become familiar with ports in the Indies and along Florida's coast.

The brigantine acquired by Narváez, typically equipped with oars, had a much shallower draft and was more maneuverable than the large ships. It served as an advance scout near coastlines and entering unfamiliar ports, taking soundings to determine entrances for the larger and deeper-draft vessels that made up the balance of the fleet. Narváez had also purchased another ship that was in the port of Havana. It was captained by Álvaro de la Cerda, with a complement of sailors, as well as forty foot-soldiers and twelve horsemen.

Narváez had been in the Indies for nearly seven months, during which time he had lost 140 men to desertion, 60 men in a hurricane, and twenty horses and two ships had been lost. He had spent the entire period going from one place to another, obtaining men, horses, and supplies, only to lose them and start over, attempting to rebuild his fleet. Finally, they were

---

117 Buckingham Smith, p. 20

ready to sail. On February 22, 1528, the Narváez fleet of four ships and one brigantine set sail from Jagua, headed for Havana to join up with Cerda's ship. With a total complement of four hundred men, ten women, and eighty horses, each of the four larger ships would have carried about twenty horses, one hundred people, and all of the other supplies needed for the two garrisons and two settlements that Narváez had agreed to establish.

Some historians have concluded that when Narváez left Cuba, he headed directly for the River of Palms. That would have made no sense. Narváez had purchased a ship with a captain and a contingent of foot-soldiers and horsemen that was in Havana. His destination when leaving Jagua would have been to go to Havana to join up with the ship commanded by Álvaro de la Cerda. Once joined with Cerda in Havana, the fleet would have consisted of a brigantine and five large ships. When united with Cerda's ship, Narváez would have had a fleet and a force approximating the one that he had left Spain with eight months earlier.

When Narváez set sail from Jagua with his fleet, he would first pass through the Yucatán channel between Mexico and Cuba in order to get to open water, then travel east to Havana. It was a total distance of about five hundred miles from Jagua, a voyage that would normally take six to eight days. After joining up with Cerda's ship in Havana, and perhaps loading more horses, supplies and men, the plan was that the ships would then set sail for Las Palmas, located about 160 miles north of Pánuco. The distance from Havana to Las Palmas was 250 leagues (750 miles), and the voyage would have been expected to take ten to twelve days.

After leaving port, Narváez's ships ran aground as they approached the western end of Cuba and were stranded for two weeks on the Canarreo shoals. This has led some historians to conclude that Miruelo must have been incompetent and had misrepresented his abilities to guide the fleet safely to their destination. An alternative explanation is that the Gulf Stream, which travels at a high velocity through the Yucatán channel, together with winds from the southwest, may have caused the ships to make "leeway." Leeway is the term used for a ship moving sideways as it sails forward. This would have resulted in the ships being farther to the east, and closer to the reefs, than the pilots thought they were. (I have personal experience in sailing to the Yucatán from Florida, but in this case, into the current of the Gulf Stream. At one point we sailed six hours at six knots and found by checking our latitude using

LORAN[118] that, while believing that we had advanced about thirty-six miles, we had actually traveled only twelve miles forward and been pushed sideways six miles off our planned track. The pilots of the 1500s did not have LORAN.) Whatever the reason for running aground, the two weeks being stranded on the Canarreo shoals was just the beginning of a nightmare voyage that had been planned to take about eight days. They sailed to the small port of Guanaguanico to effect repairs. They were hit there by a storm and "nearly shipwrecked," according to Cabeza de Vaca's account. They remained there for an unknown period, but based on the accounts of their subsequent travels, they may have been there for nearly a month. They left Guanaguanico, heading for Havana for repairs, resupply, and to join up with Cerda's ship. They encountered another storm, requiring them to stop for three days. They finally rounded the western point of Cuba and sailed against the wind, attempting to reach Havana. (The term "against the wind" meant sailing

---

118 LORAN (Long Range Navigation) was a pre-GPS navigational device that used land-based transmission towers to send signals to the LORAN unit, producing latitude and longitude. The sailor would then draw intersecting LAT/LON lines on a sea chart to determine the ship's position.

a zig-zag course, as close to the direction intended as possible.) As they approached Havana, strong winds drove them away, toward Florida.

> *We rounded Cabo de San Antón and sailed against the wind until we arrived at a point twelve leagues from Havana. And waiting another day to enter port, a south wind took us and drove us away from land. And we passed over to the coast of Florida and came to land on Tuesday, the twelfth of April, and went along the coast the way of Florida. And on Maundy Thursday we anchored on the same coast at the mouth of a bay, at the back of which we saw certain houses and habitations of Indians.*[119]

Cabeza de Vaca does not explain why, after having been aground or at sea for nearly two months, they sailed for two days before they went ashore. Since there are no mountains on the west Florida coast, land would first become visible from the topmast of a ship from 8 ½ miles offshore.[120] Even at a very slow sailing speed, land would have been three to four hours away. Why would they not seek a landing there? Cabeza de Vaca

---

119 Unless otherwise stated, all quotations from the *Relación* are taken from the translation by Adorno and Pautz.

120 MacDougald, p. 114

may not have known the reason why. He was likely not even aboard the flagship commanded by Narváez at the time, being merely a high-level passenger, with better quarters befitting his station on another ship. He most likely would not have been involved in any navigational discussions or decisions made by Narváez and his chief pilot, Miruelo, when they decided to sail to Florida, or where they had intended to go. A logical explanation is that the land that Miruelo spotted was the Dry Tortugas. He would have known that they would not find food, water, or a settlement site there. From their maps (and even more likely from his previous experience), he would have known that almost directly north of them was the Bay of Juan Ponce, about two hundred miles away.

Having reached the coast of Florida, the ships *"anchored on the same coast at the mouth of a bay."*[ii] According to the Joint Report, they "entered into a shallow bay along the coast."[121] Since, with the exception of Tampa Bay proper, all of the bays on the west coast of Florida are shallow with narrow passes

---

121 Fanny Bandelier, *The Narrative of Álvar Núñez Cabeza de Vaca*, Imprint Society, 1972. [Contained within the book is a separate section entitled *The Joint Report recorded by Gonzalo Fernández de Oviedo y Valdés*, translated by Gerald Theissen.]

flanked by sandbars and barrier islands, it would have been difficult for ships drawing ten or more feet to have entered or anchored in any of them. An anchorage outside of the relatively deeper mouth of a bay would allow the ships' service boats and their shallow draft brigantine to enter and reach the mainland. On April 14, 1528, nearly two months after leaving Jagua, a trip that had been expected to take about ten days, they had finally reached an anchorage.

Only four of Narváez's ships reached the anchorage, one of them being the brigantine. Although the expedition had left Jagua with five ships (four large ships and one brigantine), one of the ships was lost along the way. In the last chapter of the *Relación*, written by Cabeza de Vaca after he returned to Spain, he wrote that one of the ships was lost *"porque el otro era ya perdido en la costa brava"* (because the other one had been lost on the rugged coast), with no more explanation than that. The west Florida coast is not "rugged." It consists of a long line of barrier islands and mainland, all of which are fronted by shallow waters and sandy beaches. It is likely that the ship was lost when the original five ships were grounded for two weeks on the Canerreo shoals or when they were hit by a storm at Guanaguanico and "nearly shipwrecked." Since Cabeza de Vaca reported the loss of lives whenever they occurred throughout his *Relación* and did not report any in this instance, it is likely that the "lost" ship was heavily damaged and rendered unseaworthy, and that the crew and passengers, but not the horses, had been taken aboard the remaining ships.

When the ships arrived at the mouth of the bay, it had been about fifty days since they had sailed from Jagua. Thirty-eight of their horses had been lost or died along the way. They had finally arrived at an anchorage, but a tenuous one. No ship's captain wants to anchor at the mouth of a bay, as incoming and outgoing tides, storms, and strong winds could cause anchors to drag, running the ships aground. They were one thousand miles across the Gulf from Las Palmas but still within the territory defined in Narváez's charter from the king. They would have to establish their first settlements there.

Upon anchoring on Maundy Thursday (Holy Thursday), Narváez sent the controller, Alonso Enríquez, in a small boat to parlay with some Indians that he had seen on an island just inside the bay. The encounter ended after an exchange of fish and venison for some European trinkets.[iii] Narváez spent the evening aboard. The following day, Good Friday, he and a landing party went ashore to the mainland, where he had seen Indian dwellings. Upon landing, they found that the Indians had abandoned their village. Narváez and his men found a house so large that it could hold three hundred people. In the abandoned village, they found a small gold rattle. The following day, Narváez went ashore again to officially claim the land for the king.

[He] commanded the rest of the men to disembark and unload the horses that had survived, which were no more than forty-two in number because the rest had perished due to the great storms and long time at sea. And these few that remained were so thin and worn out that for the present we could make little use of them.

The horses had each been confined to a single place, supported by slings, since they had first been loaded aboard the ships. The horses were manually lifted out of the ships' holds on slings, then either lowered into the brigantine to be taken closer to shore or lowered directly into the water to swim ashore. Using his small rowboats, he shuttled his people and supplies ashore. To bring ashore forty-two sick and starving horses, four hundred men and ten women, as well as chickens, pigs, and materials needed for a settlement, must have taken a superhuman effort by the weakened would-be settlers.

The following day was Easter Sunday. No mention is made in either the *Relación* or the Joint Report of any religious observances that took place on that day, but with five priests aboard, the settlers would certainly have observed one of the holiest days of the year with a mass. They probably brought a cross from aboard ship, or constructed a cross in connection with their Good Friday and Easter Sunday observances. Cabeza de Vaca identified the place from which they had begun their journey as *de la Cruz* (Bay of the Cross) for the first and only time much later in the *Relación* when he noted the distance that he had traveled from his initial landing place.[122] Having first gone ashore on Good Friday and then celebrated Easter at their landing place, the name would be appropriate for their Boca Ciega Bay landing site. The only event reported on Easter Sunday was that a contingent of Indians came to tell Narváez that he and his men and women were not welcome. Though the would-be settlers had no interpreter, they could understand from the "many signs and threatening gestures" that the Indians wanted them to leave.

The next morning, Narváez led an expedition to discover more about his newly claimed land. He was accompanied by Cabeza de Vaca and forty men, of

---

122 Adorno and Pautz, Vol. I, p. 73

which six were on horseback. They followed a trail to the north (northeast, according to the Joint Report), arriving that evening at "the hour of vespers" (dusk) at the shore of a very large bay that extended out of sight, inland, to the north and east. Oviedo wrote that they found "*a bay that cuts into the land*," while Cabeza de Vaca described it as "*a very large bay that seemed to us to go far inland.*" They spent the night there and returned to their settlement on Boca Ciega Bay the next day. Their anchorage at the mouth of a bay was not a safe and protected anchorage for Narváez's ships, exposing them to bad weather that could cause their ships to be driven out to sea or aground. They had also not found any food and apparently not any friendly Indians. Narváez quickly determined they needed to move to another place. Cabeza de Vaca wrote, "*The governor ordered that the brigantine go along the coast toward Florida* [south[123]] *and look for the port that Miruelo, the pilot, had said he knew. In case he did not find the port, to travel to Havana and pick up Álvaro de la Cerda's ship, and after taking on some provisions, to come to search for us.*"

---

123 Adorno and Pautz, Vol. III, p. 244. "In the direction of Florida" was to travel in a clockwise direction along the Gulf coast. "In the direction of Pánuco" meant to travel in a counter-clockwise direction.

The fact that Narváez sent the brigantine looking for the port, and if he couldn't find it, on to Havana to join with Cerda's ship and return, confirms that Narváez and Miruelo knew where they were relative to the location of Havana. Miruelo would have, soon after landing, established that his latitude was about 28°N. Having been based in Cuba when Narváez had hired him, he would have known that Havana was at about 23°N, about 350 miles to the south. Assuming fair winds, the trip would take about four days each way. It would take some time for Cerda to board his horses and men, obtain additional provisions, then set sail to return. With luck, Miruelo would be back with Cerda's ship and more provisions in about two weeks.

After the brigantine had departed, Narváez once again went to the place where they had previously discovered a large bay. On this trip he took the same forty men and six horses, along with some others. This was their second trip to the "very large bay that seemed to go far inland." They did not recognize that it was today's Old Tampa Bay, and that it was connected to Tampa Bay, the very bay that they had just sent Miruelo to find. They had arrived at the south shore of Old Tampa Bay but could not see that it was connected to Tampa Bay proper, and then to the Gulf of Mexico. They were seeing a body of water extending to the north and east. They knew that their anchorage was behind them, to the south and west. It would have been illogical to assume that the large bay in front of them could somehow be connected to the Gulf of Mexico, which was located almost directly behind them. It is useful to look at a map to understand why they did not believe that bay they had found was likely the westward appendage of the bay that Miruelo had said he knew (Map 33). The direction "inland" would be to the north and east. The horizon, to a man standing at sea level, would be three miles away.[124] The width of Old Tampa Bay is twelve miles at its widest, and six miles at a midpoint along the south shoreline. To an observer reaching Old Tampa Bay from the south, the bay would appear to be going continuously inland to the north and east. The south shoreline of Old Tampa Bay would also appear to be the southern limit of the bay, extending out of sight, inland. If one could see further, one would see land. It would be impossible to see that Old Tampa Bay, six to twelve miles away, joins Tampa Bay proper, makes a sharp right turn, and leads to a pass to the Gulf of Mexico.

Once they reached the bay, they followed another

---

124 MacDougald, pp. 114–115

trail for about four leagues (ten miles) and on the way *"took four Indians."* This is the first mention of Indians since their first encounter at Boca Ciega Bay, where the Indians had gestured and given indications that they were not welcome there. That they "took" Indians indicates that hostilities had occurred, but the *Relación* and the Joint Report mention no battle. This is the first clue that the Spaniards' relationship with the Indians had been hostile from the time of their landing. The Indians had abandoned their village and had come to shout and make menacing gestures the day after Narváez had brought his people, horses, and supplies ashore. The very nature of the composition of the Narváez expedition, with an originally planned complement of ninety-two horsemen, three hundred foot-soldiers, and a substantial amount of armament, suggests that Narváez had planned to arrive at Las Palmas more as a "conquistador" than as a settler. He had demonstrated, in the conquest of Cuba in 1511–1512, that he was a ruthless conquistador who had used his superior arms to subjugate the Indians.[125]

Narváez showed these four captive Indians some maize, obviously looking for a food source. The Indians took them to their village (Tocobaga, now

---

125 Casas, p. 29

known as Safety Harbor)[126] and *"they showed us a little maize that was not yet ready to harvest."* Upon arrival at the Indian village near there, Narváez had found "many crates belonging to Castilian merchants", each containing the body of a dead man covered with a painted deerskin. They also found "pieces of linen, cloth and plumes" ("pieces of shoes and canvas, as well pieces of cloth and some iron" in the Joint Report) as well as some samples of gold. Narváez asked the Indians where the gold had come from, and they said there was none in their land, but it was plentiful far away in a place called Apalachen.

The Indians had also been asked where the boxes and artifacts had come from and *"answered by signs that they had found them in a ship that had been lost on that coast and bay."* It does not appear that historians have paid much attention to this event. A plausible explanation would be that they had been cargo boxes brought ashore by settlers and left behind, and that the scraps of shoes, linen, and iron had been taken from bodies of Europeans. If they were remnants of the Ponce de León expedition, it would also explain the immediate hostility of the natives when Narváez had first come ashore. It is also possible that the boxes

---

126 MacDougald, p.152

were remnants of a ship that sank nearby and had floated ashore or had been retrieved by the Indians, but the explanation that the Indians had found them in a ship that had been lost is the only one that the Indians, especially captives, could have been expected to give. If they had killed or driven off Europeans who had attempted to settle there, they would certainly not have told Narváez that they had.

Shipwrecks on the western coast of Florida were (and are) an uncommon occurrence. The coastal geography presents shallow water, a sandy bottom, and sandy beaches. Groundings are frequent, while shipwrecks and sinkings are not. The west coast of Florida in and around Tampa Bay does not have reefs or rocks, making a shipwreck an unlikely event. Certainly, slavers could have come ashore, unloaded cargo boxes, and then left them behind. But would slavers unload *"many crates belonging to Castilian merchants"* for a slaving expedition? Alternatively, a ship could have been lost at sea in a storm or hurricane, with cargo boxes ultimately washing ashore on one of the barrier islands bordering Boca Ciega Bay, but the discovery by the Indians of cargo boxes would not explain the immediate hostility displayed by the natives toward the Narváez expeditionaries, nor would it explain the absence of other remnants of a ship that had sunk or been driven aground. Where were the survivors? Where were the other remnants of the ship? Why only cargo boxes and a few small items of European origin?

Cabeza de Vaca, in the last chapter of his *Relación*, which was written after he had returned to Spain in 1537, for the first time wrote that the bodies they had found were "Christians." Neither the Joint Report, nor Cabeza de Vaca's own description of events at the time that they had first found the boxes from Castile mentions that the bodies were identified as Christians. Cabeza de Vaca had written:

> *There we found many crates belonging to Castilian merchants, and in each one was the body of a dead man, and the bodies were covered with painted deer hides. This seemed to the commissary to be a type of idolatry, and he burned the crates with the bodies in them.*

The Joint Report's version is similar:

> *They also found some large Castilian chests. In each of them was a dead man, and the bodies were covered with some painted hides. It appeared to them, the fray comisario and the friars, that those objects were idolatrous, and the Governor had them burned.*

It is only in the final chapter of the *Relación*, written by Cabeza de Vaca to add information that he had learned after returning to Spain, that he wrote that the ships that had gone in search of Narváez had found the same place that they had been to before: "*It was the same one that we had discovered, where we had found the crates from Castile that have previously been mentioned, in which were the bodies of the dead men, who were Christians.*"

That the bodies were determined to have been those of "Christians" at the time of the visit to the Tocobaga village is unlikely. The cargo boxes containing bodies covered with painted deerskins indicates a degree of veneration that would not be appropriate for European bodies that the Indians had found washed ashore. The fact that Narváez and his priests had them burned is stated in a very matter-of-fact way: "*this seemed to the Commissary* [Fray Juan Suárez, a Franciscan priest] *to be a type of idolatry, and he burned the crates with the bodies in them.*" Narváez and the priests accompanying him would not have ordered the bodies to be burned had they known or thought that the bodies were Christians. Cremation had always been seen as a pagan practice, forbidden by the Catholic church since its very beginning. The church's position was formally restated in a papal ruling by Pope Boniface

VIII in 1299, calling it an abomination and imposing automatic excommunication of all who chose such a procedure and of all who practiced it. The church's prohibition remained until 1983 when Canon 1176 of the Code of Canon Law began to allow it under limited conditions.[127]

The bodies found in the boxes from Castile would most likely have been those of recently deceased Indians. The burial practice of the natives at the time was to place their dead in a charnel house, and after a given period, de-flesh the corpses and bury the bones in burial mounds.[128] It was necessary to place a guard or watchman at the charnel house in order to keep the wolves from their dead. The cargo boxes had likely been re-purposed to protect the dead from scavenging animals. In *Spain's Men of the Sea*, Pérez-Mallaína describes cargo crates taken aboard ships: "the largest crates were 1.89 meters [six feet] long, by 0.84 meters [2.8 feet] wide, by 0.63 meters [2 feet] tall," virtually tailor-made to serve as coffins. The fact that the boxes and bodies were burned because they represented "a

127 Peckham, Sr Maureen. Translated from "Courrier de Rome." April 1990. *The Remnant National Catholic Newspaper.* May 2007.

128 Milanich, *Florida Indians*, p. 76

type of idolatry" would confirm that the bodies were not identified by Narváez or the priests accompanying him as Christians. It also confirms that the visit to the Tocobaga village, during which Narváez and his men burned an undoubtedly sacred place, was considerably more hostile than the *Relación* might lead a reader to believe.

The presence of "many boxes from Castile" and numerous European artifacts supports a premise that what Narváez had found were remnants of the Ponce de León settlement expedition. A Tampa Bay settlement site complies well with the location of the *Bahia de Juan Ponce* indicated on the Ribero and Colón maps, and also with the portion of it now known as Old Tampa Bay, as described by Rodrigo Rangel who accompanied the later Hernando de Soto Expedition.[129] The Ponce de León settlers surely would have brought cargo boxes ashore. In their hasty departure, known to be caused by combat with the Indians, they would have left behind their cargo boxes and their dead, providing the local Indians with items of clothing, shoes, and other artifacts. The Tocobaga Indians would also be immediately hostile to the next Europeans to attempt to settle on their shore. The maps identifying the *Bahia*

---

129 Clayton, pp. 249–254

de Juan Ponce, the Rangel description as to the location of the *Bahia de Juan Ponce* being thirty miles east of the mouth of Tampa Bay, the hostility of the Tocobagans, and the discovery of Spanish cargo boxes and items of shoes, cloth, and iron artifacts, present the only extant evidence as to the site of Juan Ponce's original colony. No evidence has been found that it may have been established at another place.

The exploration party left Safety Harbor, taking Indians as their guides, and traveled another ten or twelve leagues to another settlement. (This distance of about thirty miles, and other distances cited by Cabeza de Vaca, were written from memory when he wrote his report for the king eight years later and could be quite far off). Here they found fifteen houses and some sown plots of maize, ready to be harvested. In the Joint Report, Oviedo states that "they stayed there two days without seeing a single Indian." Two days later, Narváez and Cabeza de Vaca returned to the harbor and told the others what they had seen. Their search for food had been a failure.

The next day, on May 1, Narváez held a meeting of his subordinate officers: his Treasurer, Cabeza de Vaca; his Comptroller, Alonso Enríquez; and his Inspector, Diego de Solis. Also invited were the Commissary, Fray Juan Suárez (a Franciscan priest); a sailor,

Bartolomé Fernández (who was probably a pilot[130]); and a notary, Jerónimo de Alaniz. Narváez was seeking agreement for his proposed plan of action to move their settlement north. Narváez had sent Miruelo on or about April 18 to seek the large harbor, and if he hadn't found it to continue to Havana, join with Cerda, and return to search for them. The remaining pilots had determined that the large bay was located to their north, and that they should relocate their anchorage to it. Narváez stated that he wanted most of the men and the horses to travel inland along the coast while the ships continued along the coast, meeting at the large bay. In the subsequent discussion, as written in the Joint Report, the commissary agreed, saying that in his opinion,

> *They should go inland. They should travel staying near the coast until arriving at the harbor which the pilots said would be fifteen leagues from there, on the way to Pánuco. They would not be able to pass by without touching on this bay, because it went into the land for twelve leagues. They would wait for the ships and the ships would wait for them there.*

---

130 Adorno and Pautz, Vol. II, p. 69

The *Relación* provides virtually the same description:

> *the pilots said that going in the direction of Pánuco it would not be but ten or fifteen leagues from there, and that it was not possible, always going along the coast, for us to miss it, because they said it entered twelve leagues inland, and that the first ones to find it should wait for the others . . .*

In the following discussion, Cabeza de Vaca strongly disagreed. He said it was a very bad idea to split the ships from the land expedition, but they should instead reboard the ships, sail to the better harbor, secure their ships in a good anchorage, and establish a settlement, after which Narváez could continue his exploration from there. He argued that, "*it seemed to me that by no means should we leave the ships without first assuring that they remained in a secure and inhabited port . . . in my opinion, we should set sail and go seek a port and land better for settling.*" The notary agreed with Cabeza de Vaca, who said that "*rather than abandoning the ships, they should be left in a known and secure port and in an area that was inhabited, that once this was done, he could enter inland and do whatever seemed best to him.*" The commissary disagreed with Cabeza de Vaca, saying to reboard the ships and embark would be to "tempt God" because their entire voyage aboard ships since leaving Spain had been a disaster, with storms, groundings, and the loss of ships. The purser and the inspector agreed with the commissary and Narváez. It was a four-to-one vote with Cabeza de Vaca on the losing side. Cabeza de Vaca asked the notary to record his disagreement with the plan, and Narváez countered with a request that the notary record the fact that all of the other officers agreed with him: "*on account of there not being adequate foodstuffs in that land to establish a settlement, or a port for the ships, he was moving the settlement that he had established there and was going with it in search of the port and of land that would be better.*"

The lengthy representation by Cabeza de Vaca that he had strongly resisted the separation of the land forces from the ships was probably apocryphal. Since he was the only one who had attended the meeting that survived to tell the tale, it was his story to tell as he wished. The ultimate failure was caused by the separation of the ships from the land expedition, and Cabeza de Vaca needed to present himself to the king as the prudent leader who would have prevented the disaster had he been in charge. The real reason for the separation of the forces was likely that there was not a way to get forty-two horses back aboard the ships that were anchored outside the mouth of the bay. The brigantine, their only possible shuttle, had already left for Cuba.

Numerous books have been written by historians who have concluded that Narváez and his pilots had no idea where they were when they arrived in Florida. These assumptions are likely based on statements in the *Relación* and the Joint Report. Cabeza de Vaca wrote: "*The governor ordered that the brigantine go along the coast toward Florida and look for the port that Miruelo, the pilot, had said he knew. But he had already miscalculated and did not know where we were nor where the port was.*" Some historians have interpreted this to mean that Miruelo and his pilots had no idea where they were relative to Havana or Pánuco. One professor of history wrote a popular book about the expedition, concluding that when the Narváez expedition landed in Florida, they had thought they were in Mexico.[131] Other historians have concluded, upon reading the *Relación*, that Narváez thought that his landing place was near Pánuco (present day Tampico). This in spite of the fact that the Cortés, Ribero, and Colón maps all show Pánuco to be at the approximate midpoint of

---

131 Andrés Reséndez, *A Land So Strange*, pp. 80–87

the eastern coast of Mexico with the River of Palms to its north. Pánuco was well known to sailors of the time. It is located almost exactly on the line of the Tropic of Cancer, a line drawn on virtually every map at 23.5°N. Since four pilots remained ashore with Narváez after Miruelo had left, they had to have known that that they were at approximately 28°N and could not have believed that Pánuco was north of them.

It is not credible that pilots who certainly knew that Florida and Mexico were on opposite sides of the Gulf of Mexico, and that they were on the east side and Pánuco on the west, would have thought they were near Pánuco. It only took a look to seaward, where the sun set, to know they were in Florida and not Mexico. There is no statement in the *Relación* or the Joint Report that suggests that Narváez or his pilots or officers thought that Pánuco was nearby. The only references to moving their settlement and anchorage refer to the bay that Miruelo said he knew . . . and to a large bay extending twelve leagues inland that was "in the direction of" Pánuco and/or the Palms. There are numerous references later in the *Relación* to confirm that Cabeza de Vaca and his fellow expeditionaries had maps and certainly knew the shape of the Gulf coastline and the relationship of Pánuco and the River of Palms to their landing place in Florida.[iv] Clearly, the pilots, and even Narváez himself, knew that Mexico and the *Río de las Palmas* and Pánuco were on the east coast of Mexico and they were on the west coast of Florida. Some historians have over-emphasized the words "did not know where he was" to imply far more than what was stated in the *Relación* or the Joint Report. In essence, what they had written was that Miruelo had not arrived at the bay that he knew was nearby and went to find it. In that sense, Miruelo did not know where he was.

The meeting held by Narváez resulted in a decision to split the land force from the ships and the disastrous loss of 296 of the 300-man inland expedition. Some indication for the reasons behind that initial decision and the subsequent travels north and westward along the Gulf coast, "in the direction of the River of Palms," have been overlooked since the first English language translation of the *Relación* was accomplished by Buckingham Smith in 1851. These indications have been overlooked primarily because of a consistent error in translation and the lack of knowledge by researchers that there were two maps that had been produced before, or contemporaneously with, the start of the expedition.

The first sentence of the Relación is "*On the*

seventeenth day of the month of June 1527, Governor Pánfilo de Narváez, with the authority and mandate of Your Majesty, departed from the port of Sanlúcar de Barrameda to conquer and govern the provinces that are found from the Río de las Palmas to the cape of Florida." Although Cabeza de Vaca was referring to the River of Palms, the identification of the location of the southern boundary of Narvaez's territory had needed further clarification from the *Casa de Contratación*. The Ribero maps had two rivers with identical names, both being the *Rio de Palmas* (Maps 30 and 31). On the Colón map, drawn with the knowledge that Narváez was entitled to govern a territory that extended from the *Rio de las Palmas*, north of Pánuco, to the Cape of Florida, they had changed the name of the northernmost of the two to *Las Palmas* (Map 32). *Las Palmas* is also printed in red, while the *rio de las palmas* near the Yucatán is in black print. Red toponyms were assigned to the most important places.[132]

It is in noting the differences between the Ribero and Colón maps that a minor translation error of the *Relación* becomes apparent. In Cabeza de Vaca's description of the meeting that took place, he argued with Narváez against separating the land force from

---

132 Sandman, p. 1100

the ships. Cabeza de Vaca wrote, " ... *y que los pilotos dezian y creian que yendo la via de Palmas ...* " (that the pilots said and believed that going in the direction of the Palms). Various translations have inserted the word "river" where it does not exist in the original. When translating the statement literally, as "going in the direction of the Palms," and then identifying a place on the Colón map as "the Palms," it appears that the pilots were referring to a specific place identified on a specific map.

The pilots' certainty that there was an enormous bay to the north of them could only be based on prior knowledge from someone who had either sailed it before, seen it on maps, or had an indication in their *espejo* that it was at a particular latitude. It is possible that the pilots' certainty that a large harbor was nearby was based on incorrect information concerning the latitudes of bays on the Florida coast. Although the Colón and Ribero world maps do not show a bay north of the *Bahia de Juan Ponce*, it is possible that the maps of the Indies and the Gulf of Mexico (*padrón ordinario*) and the sailing directions that were prepared especially for Narváez by the *Casa de Contratación* did. This possibility was suggested by Jerald Milanich in *Florida Indians and the Invasion from Europe* and by Paul E. Hoffman in "Narváez and Cabeza de Vaca in Florida."[133] Both the Colón and Ribero maps have latitude scales indicated on the maps. The latitude indicated for the Bay of Juan Ponce of 27.3° is included in the *espejo* of Chavez. The date of the *espejo* is unknown but thought to be late 1520s or early 1530s. The *espejo* also identifies another bay, *Bahia Honda*, at 29°N. According to the *espejo: Bahia Honda on the west coast of Florida is at 29 degrees. This bay is large, with a length of 10 leagues and wide at the mouth 5 leagues. It has three islets in its mouth, and inside it is . . . very safe for all ships.*[134] There is no bay at 29°N, or close to that latitude, on the Florida coast. Chavez had conflated the correct description of Tampa Bay with an incorrect latitude reported by a pilot of 29°N, thus describing, and perhaps mapping for Narváez, two bays where there was only one. If Miruelo and his pilots had the *espejo*, and/or maps drawn from it, they would have believed that at 28°N they were south of a huge bay, *Bahia Honda*, extending ten leagues inland at 29°N. One degree of latitude, from 28° to 29°, was only about seventy miles, a one-day sail.

---

133 Charles M. Hudson and Carmen Chávez Tesser, *The Forgotten Centuries: Indians and Europeans in the American South*

134 Chavez, p. 366

While Miruelo was away, Narváez decided to move his ships to the north to the large bay that extended thirty miles inland, apparently believing that was where Miruelo would go to find him. He had ordered Miruelo to go south to look for the large bay, and if he failed to find it, to continue to Cuba to join up with Cerda, obtain more supplies, and return. Since Miruelo had not returned, Narváez and the other pilots would have likely concluded that the large bay must, therefore, be to the north. Narváez would have undoubtedly assumed that the very large bay would at least provide a safe anchorage for his ships and perhaps have a better food source and less-hostile Indians. When Miruelo ultimately returned to Tampa Bay with Cerda, Narváez had already departed, heading north along the coast, seeking the bay that wasn't there.

The ultimately disastrous outcome of the inland expedition would be caused by incorrect maps and latitudes provided to Narváez by the *Casa de Contratación* and the fact that Narváez and his men could not see far enough from their viewpoint on the southern shore of the "bay extending far inland," Old Tampa Bay, to recognize that it was an appendage of a much larger bay that had its mouth at the Gulf of Mexico. Narváez and his pilots must have believed that the fictitious *Bahia Honda* was just to the north and so large that it was *"not possible, always going along the coast, for us to miss it."* Tragically, the large harbor that Narváez and his land expedition would seek was not to the north, but to the south.

Narváez issued each of his 300-man land expedition two pounds of hardtack and a half-pound of salt pork and set out northward along the coast, with 42 horsemen and about 260 other men. The three ships, with a crew of one hundred and the ten wives of men on the land expedition, sailed from Boca Ciega Bay, bound for the harbor to the north, where they would rejoin with the land expedition. The ships and the land expedition would never meet again.

The land expedition traveled north along the coast for fifteen days, during which time they found no large bay with access to the Gulf, no Indians, and no food except hearts of palm. They reached a river with a very strong current and spent an entire day crossing it. They were met on the other shore by about two hundred Indians. The Indians made threatening gestures, and if hostilities ensued, they were not reported by Cabeza de Vaca. The Spaniards captured five or six of them and were led by them to some houses where there was a large quantity of maize ready to be harvested. They spent three days there, roasting corn and recovering from their near starvation. While there, the *"inspector, the controller, the commissary* [and Cabeza de Vaca] *met together, and we begged the governor to send scouts to look for the sea to see if we could find a port."* Here it becomes apparent that Cabeza de Vaca and the others believed that they must be near, or have passed, the large bay where they were to have reunited with the ships. It is possible that Narváez had a pilot with him when he went inland, as there is a reference later in the *Relación* that his pilots had determined the distance they had traveled.[135] If he did, the pilot would have used solar or star sightings to determine their position as they traveled north, perhaps seeking the port thought to be at a latitude of 29°. It may be only a coincidence that there is a river, but no bay, at that latitude. The Crystal River is located at exactly 29°N latitude, the supposed latitude of the nonexistent large bay named "Bahia Honda" that was recorded by Chavez in his *Espejo de Navegantes*. The Crystal River may be the river referred to in the *Relación*. It is one hundred miles north of Boca Ciega Bay and may have taken fifteen days to reach.

Narváez allowed Cabeza de Vaca to do a scouting mission with forty men, going back to the river that they had crossed before. They returned from their

---

135 Adorno and Pautz, Vol. I, p. 73

scouting mission to tell Narváez that they had reached the same river they had crossed before and that it might lead to a large bay, but they had been unable to cross it or follow it toward the sea. Narváez the next day sent a captain named Valenzuela with sixty foot-soldiers and six horsemen to go to the river, follow it downstream, and see if it led to a large bay. Two days later, the captain returned to report that he had found a large bay, but it had water only knee-deep, and a port could not be found. Narváez decided to continue his journey to the north. By mid-June they had found no bay and no Indians *"who dared to face us."* That was about to change.

About six weeks after they had left their anchorage, they encountered a large group of apparently friendly Indians. By sign language, Narváez indicated he was headed for Apalachen and found that the Indians there were the enemy of the local tribe. They agreed to join forces and head north together. In crossing a river, Narváez suffered his first casualty when one of his mounted horsemen, and his horse, drowned. The expeditionaries buried their comrade and ate his horse.

For the first time, and from this point on, hostilities are recounted in the *Relación,* but they are always presented as having been initiated by the Indians. They would ensue for the rest of their travels in Florida.

The following day, the Indians shot arrows at one of the Spaniards when he went to get water. A small battle ensued, and the Spaniards captured "three or four" of the Indians and took them as guides. Cabeza de Vaca at this point in his narration has recounted the "taking" of about fourteen Indians. He has never disclosed what happened to the first four Indians that they had taken near Tocobaga in his first exploration, nor the next "five or six" that they had taken fifteen days later as they marched north. He also never discloses what ultimately happens to these latest four unwilling "guides." They simply disappear from the narrative. The Joint Report and the *Relación* are the only sources of information as to what transpired in the interactions with the Indians. Narváez had been reported by Bartolomé de las Casas as being a brutal oppressor of the Indians in his conquest of Cuba in 1511–1512, and it is not unthinkable that his first encounters with the Indians of Florida would have followed a similar pattern.[136] Captain Castillo and Andrés Dorantes were both soldiers and were undoubtedly at the forefront of any combat that may

---

136 Bartolomé de las Casas, *A Short Account of the Destruction of the Indies*. Translated by Nigil Griffin. London: Penguin Books, 2004. p. 29

have taken place. They both survived to take a hand in dictating the Joint Report. It may be that they were engaged in the "taking" of the Indians and whatever hostilities may have ensued at the time and that their actions concerning their treatment of the Indians were best left unreported.

Narváez continued north, apparently unhindered by other attacks by Indians, and arrived at Apalachen, in the vicinity of Apalachee Bay (Map 18) in late June. They had found little food along the way, and most of the men were exhausted, near starvation, and "had wounds on their backs from carrying weapons on their shoulders." They came across a village, and Narváez ordered Cabeza de Vaca to attack it with nine horsemen and fifty foot-soldiers. There were only women and children there ... no warriors were to be found. As Cabeza de Vaca explored the village, the warriors attacked. They succeeded only in killing a horse, then fled. The village of forty houses contained a large supply of maize.

While Narváez occupied the village, his men undoubtedly gorging themselves on the just-killed horse and the abundant supply of maize and other foods found in the village, the Indian warriors returned to ask that their women and children be freed. Narváez agreed, keeping a chief as hostage. The Indians, having rescued their women and children, returned to attack. In the ensuing twenty-five days, small attacks continued, with the Spaniards killing two Indians and losing one of their own. They retained the captive chief, who told them there was a much bigger and better village, with more food, including maize, beans, and squash to the south, in a place called Aute. It was near the sea, with an abundant supply of fish. Narváez decided to travel to Aute. As he moved southward, he was attacked as his men crossed a lagoon in chest-deep water. The Indians *"began to shoot arrows at us in such a way that they wounded many of our men and horses."* The Indians rescued the chief that Narváez had taken as his guide. The Spaniards *"could not make use of the weapons they carried,"* as the Indians were excellent bowmen and *"can shoot arrows at two hundred paces with such skill that they never miss their target."* The Spaniards escaped from the attacking Indians and proceeded toward the coast.

The Narváez force, although exhausted and near starvation, was still not to be taken lightly. It still numbered nearly three hundred men, of which about forty were horsemen. Although the *Relación* is silent on weaponry, it is known that the foot-soldiers of the time had the crossbow and the arquebus and several close-combat weapons, including the axe, the pike, and the sword. Both the arquebus and the crossbow took considerable time to reload. The arquebus also needed gunpowder, was useless in the rain, and undependable in wet or highly humid areas. The Indians had a much more rapid rate of fire with their own standoff weapon, the bow, which could be shot several times in the time it took to cock and reload a crossbow or to reload an arquebus. The Spaniards also had horsemen equipped with lances and swords. They enjoyed a great advantage when mounted and engaging the enemy at close quarters in open environments but were at a huge disadvantage when faced by an adversary in a wooded area who could quickly fire multiple arrows and move around from tree to tree, easily outmaneuvering the horseman. The Narváez expedition was experiencing "guerilla warfare," as if the Indians had read Sun Tzu's *Art of War*. When the Spanish attacked, the Indians retreated. Where the Spanish were weak, the Indians attacked.

As the Narváez group traveled to Aute, they were once again attacked by Indians. Cabeza de Vaca and two others were wounded. When the Spaniards counter-attacked, the Indians fled and took refuge in the woods. As the group of exhausted and wounded Spaniards moved on, they were again attacked, this time from the rear. The Indians killed yet another

Spaniard, and the exhausted men carried his body a few more miles, to Aute. Upon arrival, they found the Indian's houses were burned and the people gone. They found maize and beans ready for harvest, and stayed two days, healing their wounds. Narváez ordered Cabeza de Vaca to take Captain Castillo and Andres Dorantes as well as seven other horsemen and fifty foot-soldiers to go look for the sea. This is the first mention of Castillo and Dorantes, with whom Cabeza de Vaca and Estevanico would ultimately become the only ones to survive the expedition. Cabeza de Vaca found the bay that he was seeking and many oysters, "which pleased the men very much." He spent the next few days exploring the area but found that it contained many large bays that went far inland and that the seacoast was very far from there. He returned to the Narváez encampment and found that the Indians had attacked again, killed a horse, and that many of the men in camp were wounded or sick.

The next day, the entire force went to the place Cabeza de Vaca had found earlier. It is believed to be somewhere on the shoreline of today's Apalachee Bay, south of present-day Tallahassee (Map 18). The journey was extremely difficult because the horses could not carry all of the sick and wounded. When they arrived to make camp, a near mutiny occurred when some of the horsemen decided to sneak out and abandon Narváez and the sick. It was quashed when others reported the planned treachery to Narváez. The would-be deserters were convinced that their only hope was to stay together. Narváez asked each of his men what they thought they should do. One-third of the expedition's forces were wounded or sick, and more were joining them every day. Their expedition had changed from one of exploration and conquest to one of survival.

The solution arrived at by Narváez and his men was to build boats to sail along the coast to try to get to Pánuco. This is additional evidence that Narváez had, or had seen, a map. He had moved north along the coast of Florida "in the direction of" Pánuco, indicating that he knew that his destination was in a counterclockwise direction around the Gulf coast.

There was no local source for the food that would be needed during the weeks or months that it would take to construct the boats. Individual members of the company came up with ideas as how best to proceed. For food, they would attack the local Indians to obtain maize, and they would kill a horse every third day for meat. One man made bellows from deerskins to be used to heat fires hot enough to soften their stirrups, spurs, and crossbow parts to re-form them into saws, axes, and nails. There was a Portuguese carpenter and sailor in the group, Álvaro Fernández,[137] who used the fibers and coverings from local palmettos to make oakum for their boats. (The abundant local Saw Palmetto, *Serenoa repens,* has fibers that are easy to harvest). He also made "some pipes of wood." In *Spain's Men of the Sea* the role of a ship's carpenter is described: "The carpenter was possibly one of the most indispensable specialists on board a ship . . . He played a key role, as he was responsible for fixing leaks and making other critical repairs. A ship's carpenter had to be capable of building a launch."[138] A Greek, Doroteo Teodoro, used local pines to extract pitch to use in lieu of tar to make the boats watertight. Others made ropes woven from the coverings of the palmettos and the manes and tails of the horses. They used horse hides to make containers for water. For ballast, they scoured the area and gathered rocks wherever they could find them. They used their own shirts to make sails.

Cabeza de Vaca does not describe the boats that the men built, except to say that they were about twenty-two cubits in length. It appears that a fair estimate of

---

137 Defined at this point only as a man who was "the only carpenter in the company," he is later defined as "Álvaro Fernández, a Portuguese carpenter and sailor." Adorno and Pautz, Vol. I, p. 73

138 Pérez-Mallaína, p. 80

"twenty-two cubits" is that they were thirty to thirty-five feet long. Construction continued in the ensuing seven to eight weeks, as the Indians often attacked, and the Spaniards raided villages to gather maize for their voyage. From early August until the boats were completed near the end of September, all but one of the horses had been killed and eaten. The last horse would be killed and shared among the five boats as provisions for their voyage. During the months that the boats were being constructed, more Spaniards had been killed by the Indians. "*The Indians killed ten Christians, who were fishing by these lowlands of the coast. From their base camp the Spaniards saw those unfortunate men pierced from one side to the other with arrows, but they were not able to help them.*" Another forty had died from their wounds, sickness, or starvation. Finally, in late September, five boats with 242 survivors of the original 300-man inland expedition set sail from the place that they had buried fifty of their companions and eaten their horses. They named it "The Bay of Horses."

Cabeza de Vaca wrote at this point that "*upon the declaration and oath of our pilots, from the bay that we named the Bay of the Cross to this point, we had traveled two-hundred and eighty leagues, more or less.*" This is his only reference to "The Bay of the Cross." The Joint Report's description is similar. It does not name the Bay of the Cross but cites the identical distance from the place they had left their ships. From the two descriptions, it can be determined that their landing place had been named the Bay of the Cross. The reference to the distance traveled of 280 leagues would equate to 840 miles, much farther than the distance from Boca Ciega Bay to Apalachee Bay, which was about 350 miles, even if his route had taken him well to the north and then back down to the coast. His reference to pilots is equally confusing. No mention of pilots is made in the Joint Report. Where could pilots in the Cabeza de Vaca version have come from? Narváez had sent Miruelo south from Boca Ciega Bay to look for a large harbor, and then back to Havana. He had sent his three ships north along the coast, looking for the large harbor that Narváez had not found. Each of his ships would have had at least one pilot. Perhaps Narváez had another pilot rescued from the ship that had been lost on the way from Jagua to Florida. He may have been taken inland to calculate their latitude in order to identify the large bay to the north that they were seeking. If there was a pilot on the land expedition, it would explain how they had determined where they were and why they decided to build boats to sail westward along the coast. Whether there was a pilot or not, Narváez knew that the way to Pánuco was to the west, as would become evident later in the *Relación* where Cabeza de Vaca made a number of references to seeking Pánuco by proceeding westward along the coast.

Each boat was given a captain or co-captains and loaded with about one-fifth of the company. Narváez had forty-eight men; Cabeza de Vaca and Inspector Diego de Solis had forty-seven men; the Controller Alonso Enriquez and Commissary Fray Juan Suárez had forty-six men; Captain Castillo and Andrés Dorantes (undoubtedly with Estevanico) had forty-six men; Captains Téllez and Peñalosa had forty-six men.

The 242 men on five boats set forth to sail along the shores of the Gulf of Mexico, toward Pánuco, which they thought was relatively nearby. It was actually 1,400 miles away. Soon after departing on their makeshift boats, the water bottles they had made of horse hides began to rot.

As they sailed the coast of today's Florida, Mississippi, Alabama, and Louisiana, they went ashore at many inlets and islets, looking for water and food as they moved slowly westward. Often, they found nothing. At times they encountered Indian tribes that attacked them, and at others found help from the natives to continue their journey. At one point they had gone so long without fresh water that they drank salt water, and five of the men died. Others had been killed or captured by natives along their route. Among them was Doroteo Teodoro, the Greek who had made the pitch from pine trees near the Bay of Horses to help seal their boats. He may have been the first Greek to attempt to settle in America. He and a "black" (probably his slave) were captured by Indians and never seen again.

During their journey along the coast to the west, they had reached a body of water a league wide, and "it seemed to us and we saw, it is the one they call *Espiritu Santo*."[139] This again provides evidence that they had, or had seen, a map. They obviously knew that there was a *Río del Espiritu Santo* in the direction of Pánuco, counterclockwise along the coast from their original landing place in Florida. The *Río del Espiritu Santo* is shown as a very large river opening on the Colón map, as well as on the Cortés and Ribero maps.

By November of 1528, nearly two months after departing the Bay of Horses, and seven months after landing in Florida, they had sailed the coastline nearly eight hundred miles to the west. As they neared today's Galveston Island, a severe storm struck, separating the boats. About 150 men were lost at sea. Eighty-two men were swept ashore. The survivors were widely

---

139 Adorno and Pautz, Vol. I, p.123

scattered along the Galveston and Galveston Island coastline. Many of the survivors died of starvation, illness, or were killed or enslaved by local natives. Pánfilo de Narváez drowned as he attempted to leave the island aboard one of his crudely repaired boats. The remaining Spaniards died or remained in captivity in the Galveston Island area for the ensuing six years. During his six years of enslavement/captivity, Cabeza de Vaca became a trader, traveling among the local tribes, and a medicine man using the power of prayer to cure the natives, a practice later adopted by his companions.

In 1534, six years after their original landing in Florida, four men had determined to escape: Álvar Núñez Cabeza de Vaca; Alonso del Castillo Maldonado; Andrés Dorantes de Carranza; and Estevanico. During the course of their six-year captivity, they had learned that they were the only remaining survivors of the inland expedition.

The quartet escaped captivity and headed west. The three Spaniards and the African from Morocco were likely the first men from Europe and Africa to enter the American west, proceeding inland from Galveston. Their travels west involved the first encounters between many tribes of Native Americans and the "white" and "black" man. Their survival journey took them across present-day Texas, northern Mexico, and perhaps as far north as New Mexico. On their odyssey, Estevanico had become the interpreter, learning sign and native languages. He was usually the person sent in advance, as he was the most able to communicate with the natives.

The wanderers endured incredible hardships along their journey, often naked and scrounging for the little food they found available. When they began to encounter native tribes, all four posed and were treated as powerful medicine men as they used prayer, rituals, minor surgery, and home remedies in their "healing" of the natives. They were treated as near gods in their travels west as tales of their magical healing abilities spread ahead of them. They would be escorted by one tribe to the lands of another, accompanied by hundreds of native admirers who bestowed their most-prized possessions as gifts to the four, including meat, buffalo hides, ornaments, and sacred gourd rattles. Since their escape from Galveston, they had been fed and sheltered by dozens of tribes and been treated as powerful healers, revered by the natives. There is no question that four men, traveling alone and unarmed, would have had little chance of survival but for the care and sustenance provided to them by the natives they met along their journey.

During their survival wanderings, the four travelers

had been the first Europeans, and the first African, to see and later write of the American bison and the first to report the native Indian dependence on them. Cabeza de Vaca wrote, "*These animals come from the North all the way to the coast of Florida where they scatter, crossing the land for more than 400 leagues* [1,200 miles]. *All along their range, through the valleys where they roam, people who live near there descend to live off them and take inland a great quantity of their hides.*"

In Sinaloa, Mexico, about forty miles from the Pacific Ocean, the four survivors reached salvation. They, and their large contingent of native followers, encountered fellow Spaniards who were capturing and enslaving local natives. Cabeza de Vaca ordered that the slavery be discontinued. He was told that the Spanish Viceroy and settlement were in Mexico City, one thousand miles to the south.

Native Americans had informed the four survivors of an advanced civilization of seven great cities on a trade route to the north, in an area called Cíbola. The local Indians told them of the people of Cíbola, who wore fine clothes of cotton, had much turquoise, and lived in large cities with buildings of many stories. The survivors did not attempt to find Cíbola; they turned south, to Mexico City. Upon arrival in Mexico City on July 25, 1536, the explorers had traveled more than three thousand miles over a period of eight years and three months (Map 34). Of 300 men who had landed in Florida, 296 had died or disappeared. The survivors dictated a "Joint Report," provided to Antonio de Mendoza, the Viceroy of New Spain (Mexico), including details of their eight-year journey of exploration and survival. They noted that they had heard of great rich cities in a place called Cíbola, to the north. Cabeza de Vaca returned to Spain, intent on convincing the king that he should be the next governor of *La Florida*.

Cabeza de Vaca and Hernando de Soto

On his return to Spain in 1537, Cabeza de Vaca had met with the king to recount his experiences. He learned that Hernando de Soto had recently returned as a very wealthy man from his participation in the conquest of Peru with Francisco Pizarro. Soto had been named the new *adelantado* of *La Florida*, replacing the missing Narváez. The tales told by Cabeza de Vaca to the king and Soto would have a profound impact on the Hernando de Soto expedition to follow— the longest expedition of exploration of the North American continent ever undertaken. It is very likely that Cabeza de Vaca told the king and Soto that there was likely much gold in the area of Apalachee, but that the Narváez expeditionaries had been unable to get there. Soto had urged Cabeza de Vaca to join him in his expedition to Florida, but Cabeza de Vaca declined to do so. Cabeza de Vaca sought an appointment as a governor somewhere in the New World for himself. The king agreed and appointed Cabeza de Vaca as *adelantado* of the *Río de la Plata* region (parts of today's Argentina, Paraguay, and Uruguay) in 1540, where he served until he was overthrown and sent back to Spain, perhaps in part because of his insistence on treating native Indians with kindness. This is likely due to the fact that he owed his life to the many tribes that had fed, clothed, and protected him on his earlier survival journey.

Soto proceeded to plan his settlement of *La Florida*. He certainly would have seen the 1527 Colón map, updated by other pilots returning to Seville in the twelve years since it had first been drawn. He financed a large expedition to return to the place that Cabeza de Vaca had spoken of. On February 30, 1539 (Julian calendar), Hernando de Soto landed in Tampa Bay with 500 men, 237 horses, 500 head of livestock, and 300 pigs. Upon landing, Soto encountered Juan Ortiz, a survivor of an earlier attempt to find Narváez, who had lived with the Indians for at least ten years. According to accounts of the Soto expedition written by Gonzalo Fernández de Oviedo y Valdés and others, Juan Ortiz had been captured by the chief (sometimes known as Ucita or Hirrihigua, as the name appeared in several of the Soto expedition chronicles), who had decided to kill Ortiz, but he had been saved when the chief's daughter had begged that his life be spared. Ortiz had later escaped and lived as a native with the neighboring tribe of Chief Mococo. (This was the first version of a "Pocahontas" story . . . sixty-eight years before Captain John Smith reported a similar experience at Jamestown, Virginia.) Juan Ortiz became Soto's interpreter and guide and led them as they retraced the path of Narváez's expedition northward and as they explored present-day Georgia, South Carolina, North Carolina, Tennessee, Alabama, Mississippi, Arkansas, Oklahoma, and Texas. Juan Ortiz died during the winter of 1541–1542, and Soto died near the Mississippi River, probably near present-day Ferriday, Louisiana, on May 21, 1542. The 311 surviving members of the expedition had built handmade boats on the banks of the Mississippi River and sailed downstream and into the Gulf of Mexico. They arrived in Pánuco, Mexico, in September 1543. They had traveled more than four thousand miles over a period of four years and seven months. Nearly one half of the men of the expedition had perished, and the expedition had failed to find any of the riches that they had sought.

The End of Spain's Attempts to Settle Tampa Bay

The Soto expedition had been the last attempted Spanish settlement in the Tampa Bay area of the west coast of *La Florida*. Each expedition, that of Juan Ponce de León in 1521, Pánfilo de Narváez in 1528, and Hernando de Soto in 1539, cost the lives of the men who led them.

The Tocobaga and other tribes that had been in Florida for fourteen thousand years largely died off as a result of the diseases brought there by the earliest visitors, from which the natives had no natural immunity. It would be more than two hundred years before other settlers arrived in Tampa Bay, and these arrived by land, as displaced Indians from the north moved into Florida and joined with the few remaining original inhabitants to form what is now known as the Seminole nation. Other settlers followed, first those coming by sea to establish fishing camps along the coast, and others coming later via land.

Only the ancient shell and burial mounds and a few European artifacts found buried in the ground remained as testaments to those who had lived and died during the clash of civilizations when the Old World first met the New.

Endnotes

[i] From the Chavez *espejo*:

Bahia de Juan Ponce

"Esta bahía tiene a la entrada tres isletas; a la banda del sur de ella, y a la entrada del sur por la banda del norte de estas isletas, y dentro, esta bahía es grande y limpia, y han de surgir a la banda del norte dentro en ella. Tiene a la salida de esta bahía, por la banda del norte, junto a tierra, unos islotes en rencle de luengo."

Translation by Professor Emeritus Martin Favata:

This bay has three small islands at its entrance; at its southern edge and at its southern entrance; along the northern side of these small islands and within, this bay is large and clean, and one can anchor at its northern edge. Along the northern edge [side] of its mouth, near land, it has a [long] chain of islets. *[NOTE: I used the verb "to anchor" to translate surgir. En rencle is an obsolete term that apparently means "in a line, in a chain, lined up, strung along." Luengo is an archaic term for "long." Hence my tentative translation is "a [long] chain of islets."]*

Bahia Honda

"Esta bahía es grande, tiene de luengo 10 leguas y de ancho a la boca 5 leguas. Tiene a la boca tres islotes, y dentro es limpia y bien hondable, y muy segura para todos navios. A la banda del sur, saliendo de la boca, están unos dos islotes grandes, que distarán de la boca de esta bahía 4 leguas, y al norte de esta bahia estan tambien otras tres isletas, que se dicen de San Ginés; distaran de la bahia 6 leguas."

Translation by Professor Emeritus Martin Favata:

> This bay is large—ten leagues long and five leagues wide at its mouth. It has three islets at its mouth, and within it is clean and a good place to anchor, very safe for all ships. Along its southern edge, as one leaves the mouth, there are two large islets, which will be four leagues from its mouth, and to the north of this bay, there are three other small islands called the San Ginés Islands, six leagues from the bay. [NOTE: Chavez writes "es...bien hondable." Hondable is closely related to hondear, a variant of fondear, which can mean "to measure depth" but is readily given as a specific nautical term meaning "to anchor." The verb distar, fairly common in Spanish, is one of those that apparently has no exact equivalent in English. Examples: "Orlando no dista mucho de Tampa" = "Orlando is not a long distance from Tampa," or "Orlando is not far from Tampa." Another example: "Atlanta dista 400 millas [miles] de Tampa."

ii The word *surgir* is not used in modern times for "anchor." The sentence in the *Relación* relating to their place of arrival reads: "*y Jueves Sancto surgimos en la misma costa en la boca de una baía...*" Sterling Professor Rolena Adorno of Yale University has translated the sentence as, "And on Maundy

Thursday we anchored on the same coast at the mouth of a bay . . . " The translation of *"surgimos* as "anchored" is explained by Adorno as follows: *"Surgimos*: In Gothic of black-letter typeface, the word is identical in both the 1542 and 1555 editions: *surgimos.*" We translated the verb as "we anchored" because the verb *surgir* has an earlier meaning and usage than one commonly found in twentieth-century dictionaries. I will transcribe the Spanish and then translate it. My source is María Moliner, *Diccionario de uso del español*, 2 vols., 2da. ed., Madrid: Gredos, 2002, vol. 1, p. 1322b: *"Surgir: antiguamente, 'fondear': Uso marítimo: 'Fijar un barco en un sitio echando el ancla o pesos que descansen en el fondo > anclar, echar el ancla [o las anclas]"'*: "In maritime terms, *fondear* means to cast an anchor; the literal translation of the dictionary phrase is 'to fix a seacraft in a place by casting an anchor or weights that rest at the bottom > to anchor, to cast an anchor, or anchors." Thus we translated as "we anchored."

This definition of *surgir* is supported in the *Espejo de Navegantes* of Chavez, where he used the word *surgir* in numerous entries to indicate anchorages. Example: P.361, under *Río de Palmas*: *"En el puerto pueden surgir navios . . . "* (In the port you can anchor ships).

The anchorage by Narváez at the "mouth" of a bay means that the larger ships were anchored offshore as close as they could get their deepest-draft vessels to the entrance to the bay.

iii There may be archaeological evidence of this event, hidden away in the coffers of the Smithsonian. Just inside Boca Ciega Bay is an island with an Indian burial mound on it that was created long before the Narváez expedition. In the Annual

Report to the Smithsonian Institution—1879, S. T. Walker wrote of archaeological work that he had done in the spring and summer of that year. Under the heading "Burial Mound at John's Pass" (the modern name of the main pass into Boca Ciega Bay, which has migrated northward due to a hurricane in 1848), he wrote:

> Here on a low mangrove island just inside the pass, lying east and west, is a small burial mound. . . . The mound had never been explored, but many bones and skulls lay exposed upon the surface, the result of weathering, or perhaps of invasions by the sea, or both. . . . The whole foundation of the mound was covered with broken pottery previous to the internment of any of the bodies. . . . I succeeded in obtaining nine perfect crania from this mound, among these several children, <u>but no ornaments except a</u> <u>solitary glass bead and a short tube of silver formed by rolling a thin plate</u> <u>into a cylinder</u>.

iv There are numerous references in the *Relación* that indicate that Narváez and his pilots had a map or knew the locations of Florida and Mexico from previous experience sailing in the Indies. Miruelo certainly would have known that *La Florida* was north of Cuba and that Pánuco and the *Río de las Palmas* were in Mexico. The first references to traveling "in the direction of" Panuco and/or the River of Palms occur during the meeting in which Narváez decided to travel north to seek a large bay. One reference occurs when Narváez had called a meeting to say that the pilots *"said and believed that going in the direction of las Palmas,"* they were very close to the large port. In the same meeting, the commissary, Fray Juan Suárez, had said, *"Always going along the coast, they should go in search of the port (because the pilots said that going in the direction of Pánuco it would not be but ten or fifteen leagues from there, and that it was not possible, always going along the coast, for us to miss it, because they said it entered twelve leagues inland), and that the first ones to find it should wait for the others . . .* " Some have interpreted this to mean that the pilots thought that Pánuco and the River of Palms were just to the north because the structure of the sentence can be misunderstood. By using the operative words "they should go in search of the port . . . in the direction of Pánuco . . . and was not possible to miss it." The word "it" means that the huge bay reaching far inland, and not Pánuco, was the port they sought. Pánuco was well known to sailors and mapmakers at the time. It is located almost exactly on the line of the Tropic of Cancer, a line drawn on virtually every map at 23.5°N. Since the pilots had to have known that they were at approximately 28°N, they could not have believed that Pánuco was north of them. They also knew that Pánuco was on the west side of the Gulf and Florida on the east. They could not have had sailing directions or maps that showed a huge bay on the east coast of Mexico, as there is nothing resembling a huge bay on the entire east coast of Mexico. Neither Pánuco, the *Rio de las Palmas*, nor any other port on the eastern coast of Mexico in any way resembles a deep bay reaching twelve leagues inland. That Narváez and his pilots had maps is supported in numerous future directional references in the *Relación*. During their survival journey, they had built boats to sail westward along the Gulf coast. Cabeza de Vaca wrote, "*we again took up our journey along the coast in the direction of the Río de Palmas.*" Upon seeing a large river, Cabeza de Vaca wrote, "*we arrived at an inlet a mile wide . . . it seemed to us . . . it is the one called Espiritu Santo* [Mississippi River]." After being swept ashore near Galveston, "*we agreed that the healthy men should go to Pánuco.*" During their captivity, "*Méndez had fled, going along the route toward Pánuco.*" Later, "*He* [Figueroa] *urged us to come with him to go together along the route to Pánuco.*"

Maps

As is described in the text, large-scale maps when reproduced in books prevent toponyms from being read. Most maps in the following section are enlargements of relevant portions of the maps cited. The very large Colón and Ribero maps are shown in their entirety in order to demonstrate both the scale of the areas covered in the originals and the difficulty of reading any but the largest legends and toponyms. Selected areas around the Gulf of Mexico have also been significantly enlarged so that toponyms can be read.

SPECIAL NOTE: High resolution scans of the 1527 Colón and 1529 Ribero maps as provided by Johann Georg Kohl in *Die Beiden Ältesten General-Karten von Amerika* of 1860 have been provided to the University of Florida and are now available online at the University of Florida's George A. Smathers Digital Collection. The 1527 Colón map is at : https://ufdc.ufl.edu/l/AA00080764/00001 The 1529 Ribero map is at : https://ufdc.ufl.edu/l/AA00080765/00001

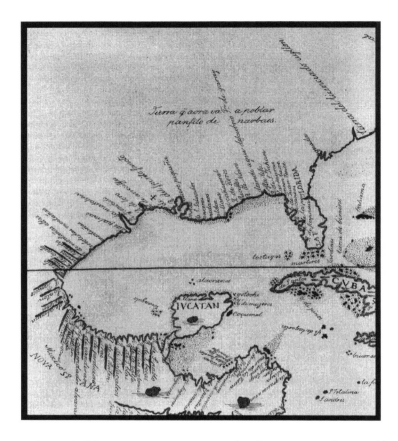

1. USLC Colón Map—1527. Detail of Mexico, the Gulf of
Mexico, and Caribbean section of the 1527 world map titled
*Carta universal en que se contiene todo lo que descubr[ieron]
del mundo sea fasta aora*, known as the Hernando Colón
map. USLC, Geography and Map Division, Johann Georg
Kohl Collection, no. 38. This map launched the effort to find
the full-scale original, as it identifies "lands that Panfilo de
Narbaez is now going to populate," and the *b. de Juan Ponce*.
Image from *Álvar Núñez Cabeza de Vaca: His Account, His
Life, and the Expedition of Pánfilo de Narváez* by Adorno and
Pautz. Volume 2, p.36.

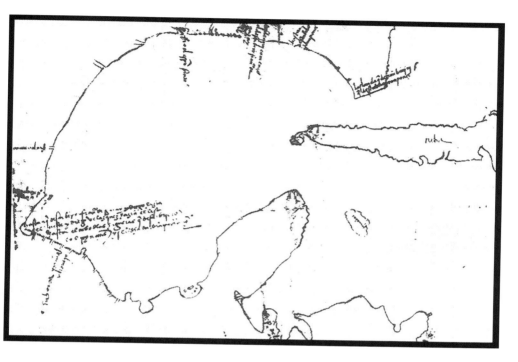

2. Pineda—1519. Alonso Álvarez de Pineda map of Gulf of Mexico. Note two dots on the Florida coast, probably representing Charlotte Harbor and Tampa Bay. North of the dots, in the vicinity of Apalachee Bay, is written, "to here was discovered by Juan Ponce." Archivo General de Indias, Seville.

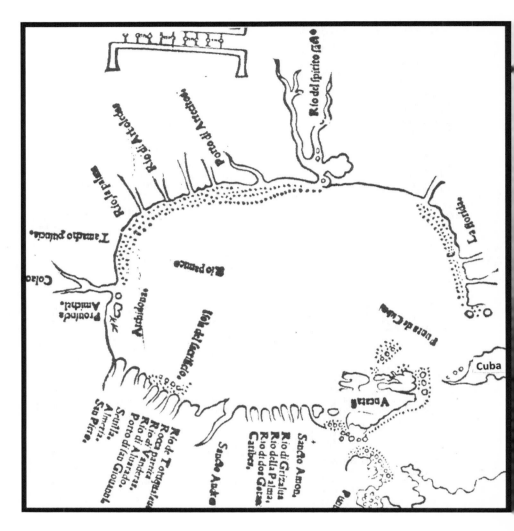

3. Cortés—1520. Hernán Cortés map of the Gulf of Mexico. Has *Rio, la Palma* north of *Rio Panuco*, and a *Rio, della Palma* near the Yucatán. The original 1520 map as provided by Cortés to the king has been lost. It was copied as a woodcut and printed in Nuremberg in 1524. Image from *Boldly Onward* by Lindsey Williams.

4. Cantino Planisphere—c. 1502. Detail. Shows today's Hispaniola, Cuba, Florida, and coast of Yucatán peninsula. Image from Nordenskiöld, 1889. Biblio Estense, Modena, Italy.

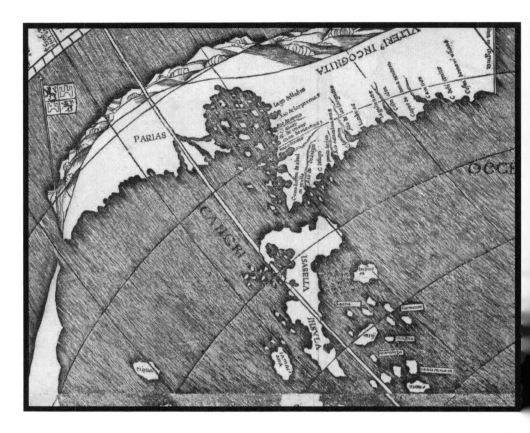

5. Waldseemüller—1507. Detail. Shows present-day Cuba and Florida. Shows shape of Gulf of Mexico and connection of Florida to landmass surrounding Gulf of Mexico. Produced twelve years before its "discovery" by Pineda in 1519. Also shows gap between today's North and South America. Image from Nordenskiöld, 1889.

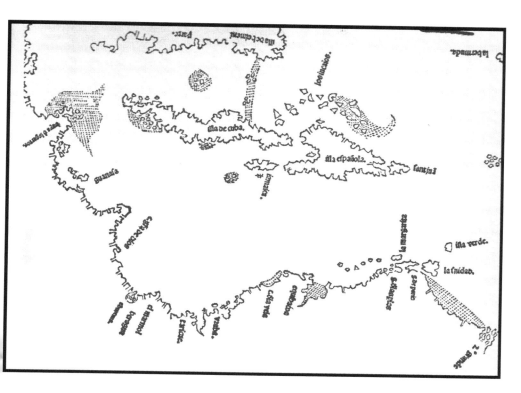

6. *Angli mediolansis opera.* Peter Martyr de Anghiera—1511.
Shows Española and Cuba, with Florida north of Cuba.
Landmass extends west of Florida, but no connection made
to landmass of what is now Mexico. May have led to belief
that a sea passage existed in that area. Also shows present-
day Mexico coast. University Library, Bologna. Image from
Nordenskiöld, 1889.

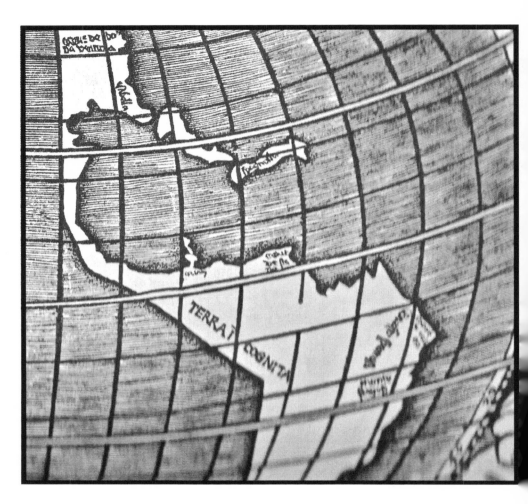

7. *Introductio in Ptholomei Cosmographiam.* Strobnicza—1512. Detail. Shows North and South America connected and a sea to the west, a year before its "discovery" by Balboa in 1513. Shows Hispaniola and Cuba, with Florida north of Cuba. Florida is connected to the landmass surrounding Gulf of Mexico. Produced seven years before its "discovery" by Pineda in 1519. Image from Nordenskiöld, 1889.

8. *Tabula Oceani Occidentalis seu Terra Nove.* Argentinae—1513.
Detail. Shows *Spagnola* (Hispaniola) and *Isabella* (Cuba)
and Florida as *Coniello*. Florida is connected to the landmass
surrounding the Gulf of Mexico. Produced six years before
Pineda "discovery" that Florida was connected to Mexico, in
1519. Image from Nordenskiöld, 1889.

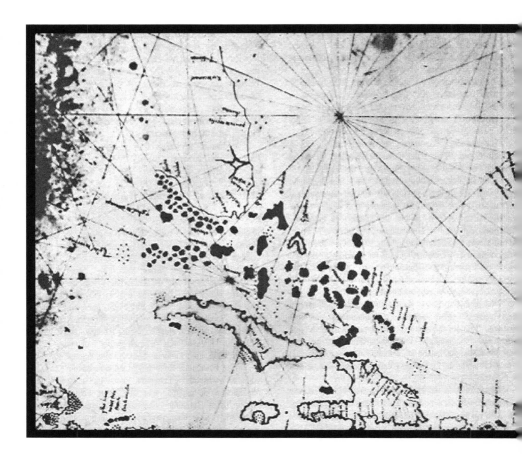

9. *Carta Nautica di Conte Ottomano Freducci d'Ancona*—c. 1514. Detail. This map contains a toponym for *La Florida* on the northeastern coast of Florida. This map likely indicates the coastline of *La Florida* as observed by Ponce de León on his 1513 discovery expedition. It was described in detail by David True in *The Freducci Map of 1514–1515* and by Jerald Milanich in "Revisiting the Freducci Map: A Description of Ponce de León's 1513 Florida Voyage?" Original in National Archives, Florence.

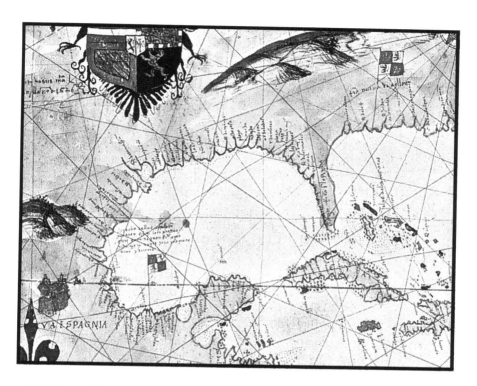

10. Juan Vespucci World Map—1526. Detail. *Ju[an] Vespuchi pilato desus ma[jes]ta me fezit en seuilla [a]ño d[e] 1526.* (Juan Vespuchi, his majesty's pilot made me in Seville in the year of 1526). Signed and dated at top left near Spanish shield. Contains legend and Spanish flag near present-day South Carolina coast, "New Territory of Ayllón." Thought by many to be a copy of the official *Padron Real.* Drawn in the year of Ayllón's ill-fated 1526 settlement expedition. Note that it shows the Martires extending westward to the Tortugas, showing that a safe passage to Florida would be to stay west of the Tortugas before turning toward the Florida coast. Oddly, it resembles neither the Colón nor Ribero maps as to the shape of Florida or the toponyms contained on it. Hispanic Society of America, New York.

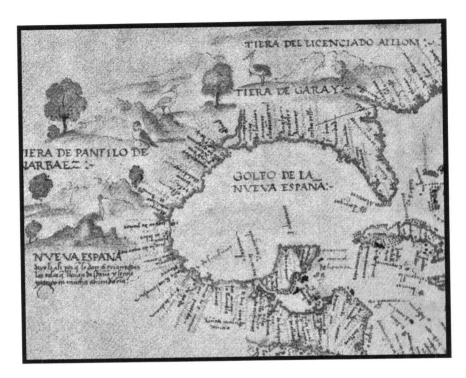

11. *Carta de América y Filipinas en dos partes* by Alonso de
Chavez c. 1532. Also known as the Wolfenbüttel-Spanish
map. Detail. Note that it indicates *Tiera de Garay* (who
died in 1523) adjoining *Tiera de Panfilo de Narbaes,* who
was assigned the rights to the lands previously assigned to
Garay in December 1526. The *Tiera de Panfilo de Narbaes* is
shown too far to the west. Thought, incorrectly, by some to
have been drawn in 1527 because of identification of *Tierra
de Panfilo de Narbaes.* Merás argues convincingly that it
must have been drawn after 1530, based on toponyms on
the map. News of Narvaez's death did not reach Spain until
1536. There is no time that attribution to those territories
simultaneously to Garay and Narváez would have been
correct. Herzog August Bibliotheck, Wolfenbüttel.

12. *Carta Universal en que Se contiene todo lo que del mondo Se ha descubierto fasta agora: hizola Diego Ribero cosmographo de Su magestad: Año de 1529. ẽ Sevilla: La qual Se devide en dos partes conforme A la capitulacion que hizieron los catholicos Reyes de españa, y elrrey don Juan de portogual En Tordesillas: Año de 1494.* Diego Ribero—1529. Also known as the "Propaganda Map." Detail. Only one-fourth of the map, which measures in total 33" x 84" is shown above. Assigns the territory on north coast of Gulf of Mexico to Garay. This version of the map was reproduced from the original in the Museum of the Propaganda in Rome. Lent by His Holiness Pope Leo XIII to W. Griggs, London, and copied in 1889. The author believes this to be the last *Padrón Real*, which became obsolete in 1526 and was highly decorated and given or sold to Marquis Agostino Chigi in 1529. See Appendix VIII. Library of Congress.

13. *Carta universal en que se contiene todo del mundo se ha descubierto fasta agora, hizola diego Ribero cosmographo de su magestatd ano de 1529.* Diego Ribero—1529. Only the Americas portion was copied by Kohl, representing one-fourth of the *carta universal.* Nearly identical to Propaganda map, but there are some variations. (See Appendix V.) Note latitude scale on right side of map. Assigns territory on north coast of Gulf of Mexico to Garay. Note many detailed legends not included on Colón map. Words on maps underneath ship drawings in the Atlantic say "to the Indies" and "from the Indies." Provided with publication by Johann Georg Kohl in *Die beiden altesten General-Karten von America Ausgeführt in den Jahren 1527 und 1529.* Published in *1860.* Personal collection of the author.

14. *Carta Universal en que se contiene todo lo que en el mundo se a descub(ierto) fasta aora. Hizola un cosmógrafo de S.M. Anno MDXXVII.* Attributed to Hernando Colón—1527. Only the Americas portion was copied by Kohl, representing one-fourth of the *carta universal*. See cover for color version. Note latitude scale on right side of map. Assigns territory on north coast of Gulf of Mexico to Narváez, eliminating reference to Garay. Note that map lacks detailed illustrations and legends contained on the Ribero maps. Provided with publication by Johann Georg Kohl in *Die beiden altesten General-Karten von Amerika Ausgeführt in den Jahren 1527 und 1529*. Published in 1860. Author believes this is the first *Padrón General*, produced on orders from King Carlos I in 1526. Personal collection of the author.

15. Ribero/Propaganda—1529. Detail. Note *Tiera de Garay*. Garay died in 1523, and his territories were assigned to Narváez in December 1526. Also note large legend *Tiera de Ayllón*. Bay of Juan Ponce appears for first time on a map.

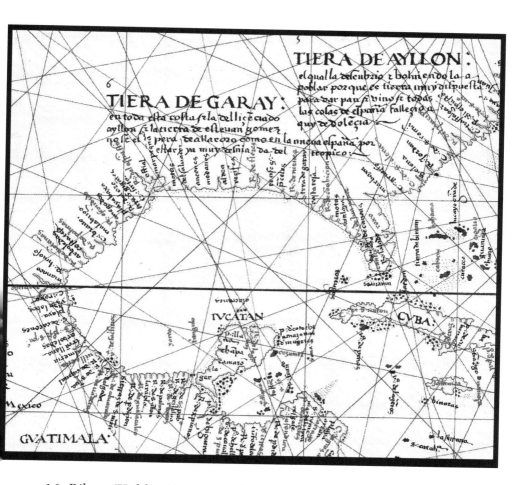

16. Ribero/Kohl—1529. Detail. Note *Tiera de Garay*, whose territory was assigned to Narváez in December 1526, as well as *Tiera de Ayllón*, who died in the winter of 1526. Bay of Juan Ponce first appears on this and Propaganda map. Note that it is nearly identical to the "Propaganda Map" (Map 15).

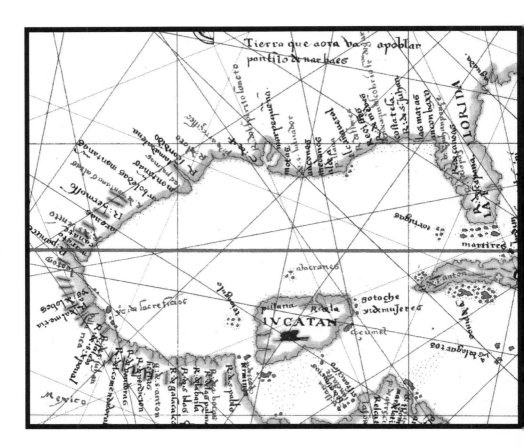

17. Colón/Kohl—1527. Detail. Note *Tierra de Garay* is replaced
with *Tierra que aora ba apoblar panfilo de narbaes*. Small
inscription in red slightly west of the Florida panhandle says,
"*donde aqui descubrío fr de garay*." The *B. de Juhan ponce*
is in red and is due north of *tortugas*. Note shape of Gulf
is elongated as compared with Ribero maps. See cover for
color rendition.

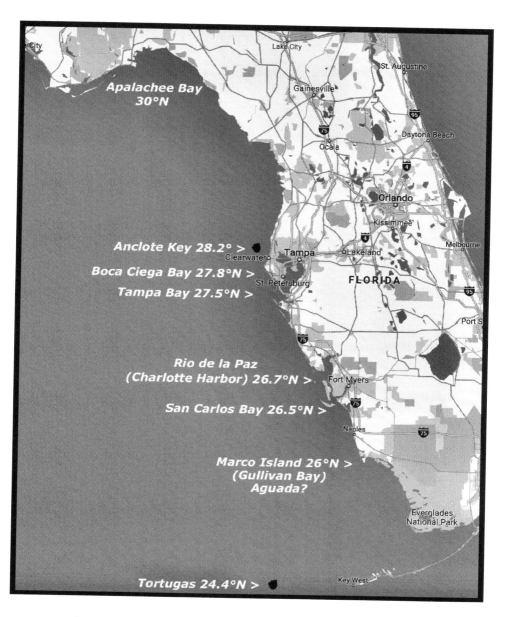

18. Florida Orientation. Place names and latitudes. Map by
author. Google Maps. Google. 21 April 2020. Web.

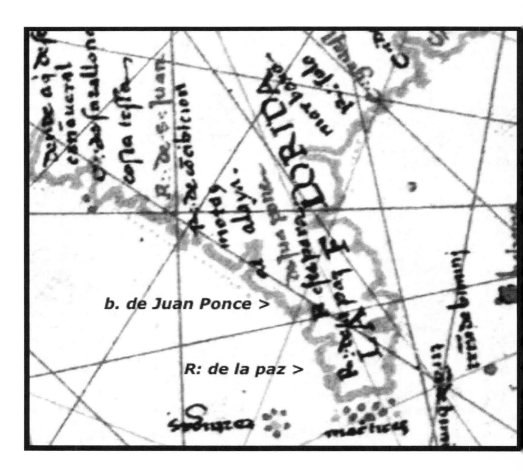

19. Ribero/Propaganda—1529. Detail. This extreme enlargement shows the *b de Juan Ponce* north of *R de la Paz*. The *b de Juan Ponce* is in red.

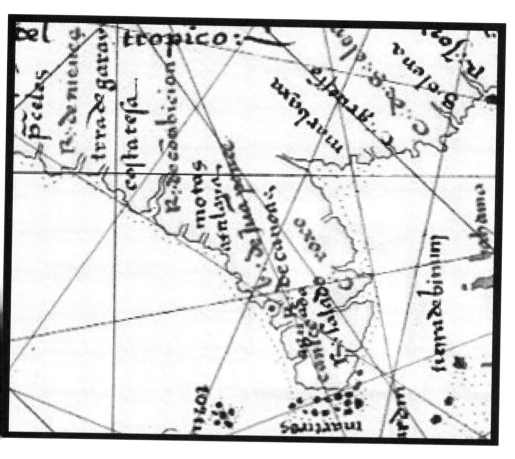

20. Ribero/Kohl 1529—Detail. *B. de juan ponce* shown north of
    r. de canoas. Below are *aguado* and *canico*.

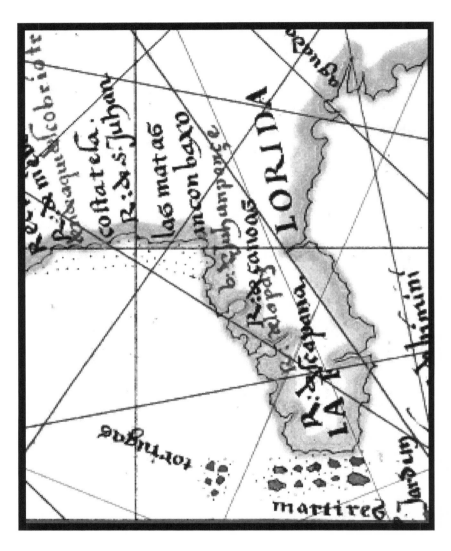

21. Colón/Kohl—1527. Detail of Florida with toponyms. Waterways from south to north are *r. de escapana, r. de la paz,* and *r. de canoas.* North of *r. de canoas* is *b. Juhan ponce.* The Bay of Juan Ponce is shown directly north of the Tortugas.

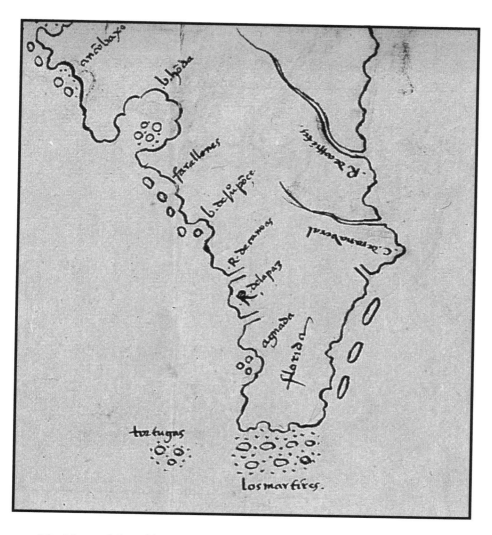

22. *Mapa del Golfo de la Nueva España; desde el Río de Pánuco hasta el cabo de Santa Elena.* Alonso de Santa Cruz c. 1554. Detail of Florida with toponyms. Southernmost is *R. delapaz.* North of it is *R. decanoas.* North of *R. decanoas* is *b. de Jupoce.* Original at *Archivo General de Indias*, Seville. Library of Congress.

23. "De Soto Map"—Gerónimo de Chavez c. 1544. Enlarged detail of Florida with toponyms. Believed to have been drawn from description by Gentleman of Elvas, a survivor of the Soto expedition. *Río de pas* is southernmost river. North of it is *Río de Canoas*. North of *Río de Canoas* is *Juan de Ponce*. Shape of *Juan de Ponce* is shown, indicating a northern appendage. Note latitude scale, placing Bay of Juan Ponce at approximately 27°N and *Rio de pas* at 25°N, separated by *R. de canoas*. The *Baya de Sp*[irit]*u* Santo, the name given by Hernando de Soto to today's Tampa Bay, is drawn at approximately 29°N, where there is no bay. First published in Abraham Ortelius *Theatrum Orbis Terrarum.* 1584.

24. T. G. Bradford—1835. The Pease River enters Charlotte
Harbor from the north. The Caloosahatchee River is named
the Charlotte River on this map. *Comprehensive Atlas—
Geographical, Historical, and Commercial.* Thomas G.
Bradford. Boston: 1835. Personal collection of the author.

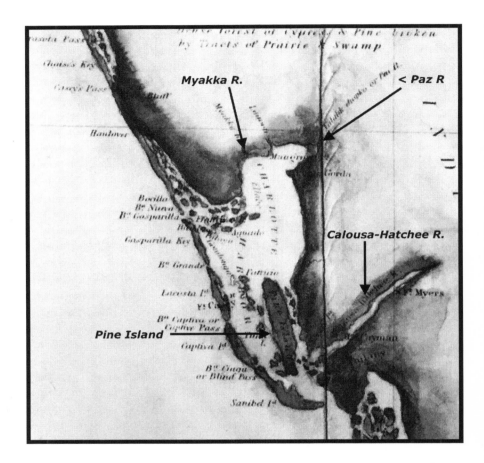

25. U.S. Coastal Survey Map, 1848–1851—A.D. Bache,
Superintendent. Detail. Note "Paz R." indicated at top right
of map. This map, drawn 320 years after the Colón and
Ribero maps, may be the last to use the name "Paz" for the
river that enters Charlotte Harbor from the north. Note Pine
Island, just north of Sanibel Island. Also note barrier islands
protecting entry into Charlotte Harbor. Sailing directions
printed on this map say the deepest pass available to enter
Charlotte Harbor, Boca Grande, was twelve feet. Personal
collection of the author.

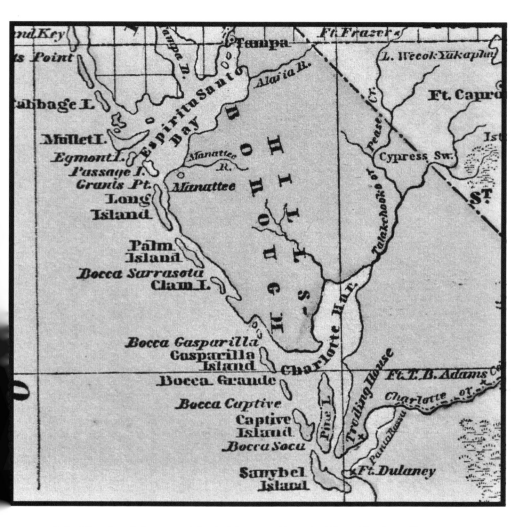

26. Charles Morse—1856. Tampa Bay is identified as Espiritu Santo Bay, with "Tampa B." an appendage to the northeast from its entrance. The river going north from Charlotte Harbor is labeled as the Talakchooko or Pease Creek. *Morse's General Atlas of the World.* New York: D. Appleton and Company, 1856. Personal collection of the author.

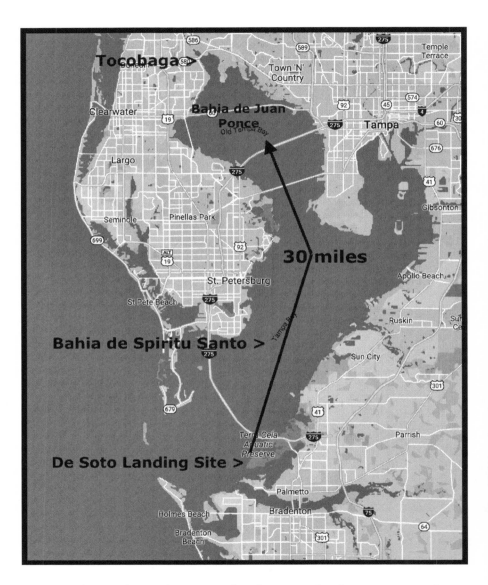

27. Relationship of Hernando de Soto landing site to the
    Bay of Juan Ponce, as described by Rodrigo Rangel, who
    accompanied the Hernando de Soto Expedition in 1539.
    Map by author. Google Maps. Google. 21 April 2020. Web.

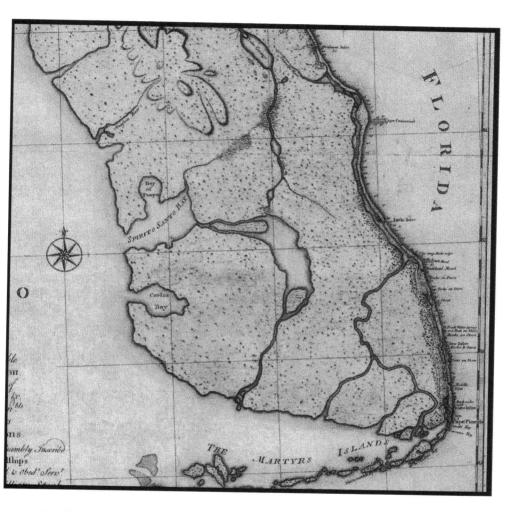

28. New Map of East Florida—William Stork—1767. Florida was acquired by England in 1763. Tampa Bay is shown as Spirito Santo Bay, with Bay of Tampa an appendage to the northeast of the main bay's entrance. What later became Charlotte Harbor is identified as Carlos Bay, well to the south of Spirito Santo Bay. Touchton Map Library, Tampa Bay History Center.

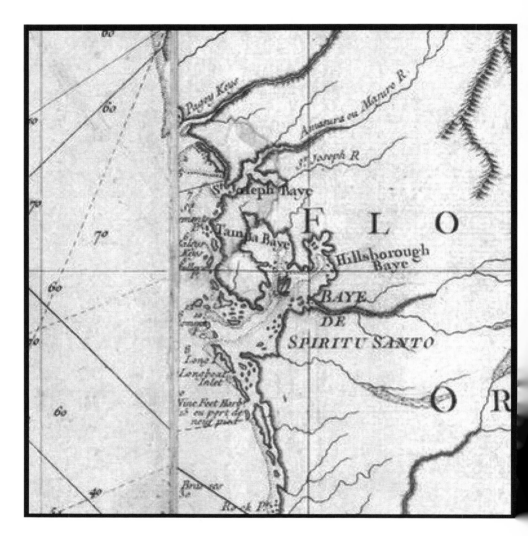

29. George-Louis Le Rouge—c. 1774. *Carte de la Floride occidentale et Louisiane.* Today's Tampa Bay is shown as the Baye de Spiritu Santo, with Tampa Baye an appendage to the northeast of the main bay's opening. Taken from Atlas amériquain septentrional 1778–1791. Paris: Chez Le Rouge, 1791. U.S. Library of Congress.

30. Ribero/Propaganda —1529. Detail. Key toponyms are in red on a yellow background, making them difficult to discern when rendered in black and white. Unlike the Cortés map, which had two rivers with similar names, *Río la Palma* and *Río della Palma* (Map 3). This map now has the two rivers with identical names. When Narváez was appointed *adelantado* of all lands from the *Rio de las Palmas* to the Cape of Florida, these toponyms would have to be changed to eliminate confusion. The *Bahia de Juan Ponce* appears for the first time on this map.

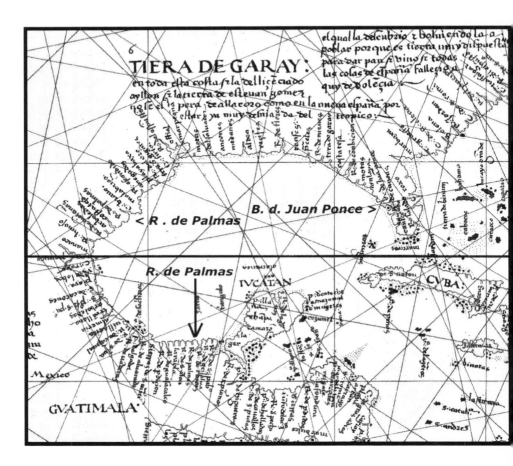

31. Ribero/Kohl—1529. Detail. Note identical river names, *r. de Palmas*. The *B. de Juan Ponce* is shown for first time on a map.

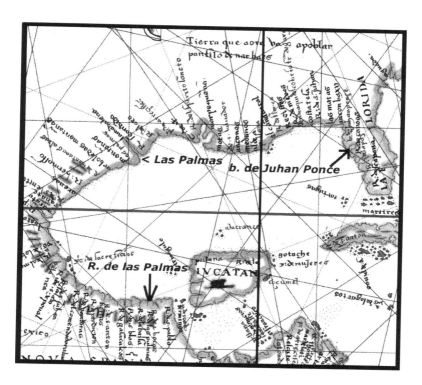

32. Colón/Kohl—1527. Detail. Note that this map prepared for
Narváez has river names changed from Ribero versions so
that they are no longer identical. The northern one becomes
las palmas, in red, and the southern one to *R de las palmas,*
in black. Also, what was labled as *r. de montañas* on the
Ribero maps is now identified simply as *montañas,* just
south of *Las Palmas,* which may have been done to provide
a navigational aid. The *b. de Juhan Ponce* is also shown on
this map in red. (See cover). Note accurate shape of Florida,
rarely seen on other maps. Also, inaccurate shape of Gulf,
making *Las Palmas* appear to be on north coast of Gulf,
about two hundred miles north of its actual position. Heavy
line across map is the Tropic of Cancer, which crosses north
of Pánuco.

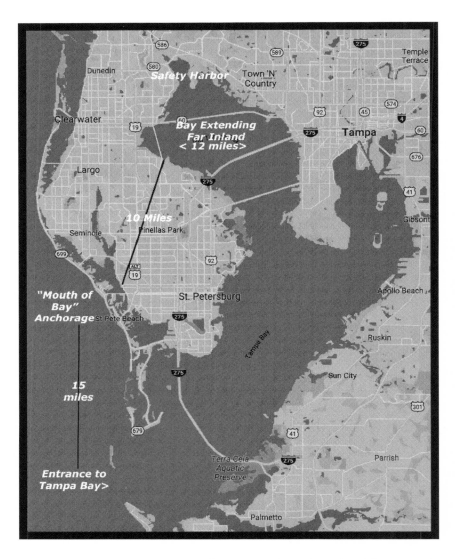

33. Narváez landing site and "bay extending far inland." It would have been impossible to see from the southern shoreline of Old Tampa Bay that it had a connection to the Gulf. Map by author based on descriptions in *Relación* and Joint Report. Google Maps. Google. 15 April 2020. Web.

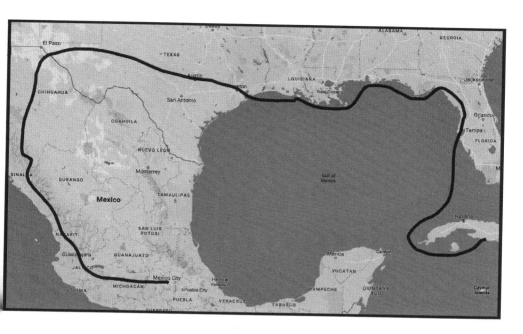

34. Approximate route of the Narváez Expedition. Narváez left Cuba in February 1528. He separated his ships from his land expedition after landing in Boca Ciega Bay near Tampa Bay in April. The three hundred men of the land expedition traveled north along the coast until reaching Apalachee Bay. They built boats and sailed the coast to the Galveston Island vicinity. Narváez died there. The survivors were taken captive or killed by the local Indians. Six years later, the only four survivors, Álvar Núñez Cabeza de Vaca, Alonso del Castillo Maldonado, Andrés Dorantes de Carranza, and Estevanico, escaped and went inland, reaching Sinaloa about eight years after landing in Florida. They then traveled another thousand miles, reaching Mexico City in July 1536. Map of route by the author. Google Maps. Google. 14 July 2020. Web.

APPENDIX I

The *Relación* and the Joint Report– Primary Sources

Two primary references are used in the study of the Narváez expedition. The most cited is the *Relación*, written by Álvar Núñez Cabeza de Vaca, one of only four survivors of the three-hundred-man inland expedition. Cabeza de Vaca wrote a report to the king when he returned to Spain in 1537, known in short as the *Relación*. It was published as a book in Zamora 1542 under the title *La relacion que dio Alvar Núñez cabeça de vaca de lo acaescido en las Indias en la armada donde yua por gouernador Pamphilo de narbaez desde el año de veynte y siete hasta el año de treynta y seies que boluio a Seuilla con tres de sus compañia* (The account that Alvar Núñez Cabeza de Vaca gave of what occurred in the Indies on the expedition of which Pánfilo de Narváez served as governor, from the year of [fifteen] twenty-seven until the year of [fifteen] thirty-six, when he returned to Seville with three members of his company). A second version was published in 1555 in Valladolid, basically unchanged as to the relation of the Narváez expedition but changing the title to *La relacion y comentarios del gouernador Aluar nuñez cabeça de vaca, de lo acaescido en las dos jornados que hizo a las Indias*. In this edition he adds his account of his second journey to the New World, this time as *adelantado* of the *Rio de la Plata* region, parts of today's Argentina, Uruguay, and Paraguay.

The second primary source of information relating to the Narváez expedition is the "Joint Report," dictated to the scribes of the Viceroy of New Spain and signed by the three Spanish survivors of the expedition, Cabeza de Vaca, Alonso del Castillo Maldonado, and Andrés Dorantes when they arrived in Mexico City in 1536. A number of copies of the Joint Report were made at the time it was dictated. One was for Cabeza de Vaca for his use in writing his own longer and more detailed version, the *Relación*, meant for the king. Another was prepared for the Council of the Indies in Hispaniola. Perhaps another was made for the Viceroy of New Spain, whose scribes undoubtedly created the written report. Although the original report has been lost, a noted chronicler of the exploration and conquest of the New World,

Gonzalo Fernández Oviedo y Valdés (Oviedo) had a copy and included it as chapters one through six in book thirty-five of his enormous multivolume work, the *Historia General Y Natural De Las Indias: Islas Tierrafirme De Mar Oceano*. In it Oviedo wrote, "*The chronicler* [Oviedo] *took this relation from the letter these gentlemen sent to the Audiencia Real which resides in this city of Santo Domingo on this island of Española*." It is apparent from this statement that the Oviedo version may have been only a summary of the Joint Report, in that he says he "took this relation from" the letter sent by Cabeza de Vaca, Dorantes, and Castillo. It also includes, in parentheses, Oviedo's opinion in various places. This version of the Joint Report and the *Relación* have become the primary information sources used for centuries by scholars and historians. Information from these publications has been supported and augmented by reviewing writings of other chroniclers of the era and copies of letters that were written by various officials of the time.

Any study of the Narváez expedition must include a careful comparison of both the Joint Report and the *Relación*. The Joint Report, having been dictated and signed by the three Spanish survivors, would be the most reliable source and could serve to confirm or contradict what Cabeza de Vaca wrote in his own much-expanded version. In order to confirm or supplement Cabeza de Vaca's representations, the Oviedo summary of the Joint Report must be compared with the *Relación*, paragraph by paragraph, to see whether there are any significant differences. There are many differences, but none that do not support the underlying truths of the Cabeza de Vaca account. Cabeza de Vaca offers far more detail, especially regarding the names of men on the expedition and the names of the Indian tribes that he encountered in his travels. He also offers expanded, or slightly different, descriptions of his location at various times. One example is that he wrote that they "anchored in the mouth of a bay," while the Joint Report says that they "entered into a shallow bay." In another example, in recounting the direction traveled on their first inland foray, Cabeza de Vaca wrote "north," and Oviedo "northeast."

A comparison of seven English translations of the *Relación* resulted in a determination that there was general consistency among them. It appeared that reliable and well-explained translations were contained in *Álvar Núñez Cabeza de Vaca: His Account, His Life, and the Expedition of Panfilo de Narváez* by Adorno and Pautz, and in *The Account: Álvar Núñez Cabeza de*

Vaca's Relación by Favata and Fernández, which have been employed as "master versions."

The Oviedo summary of the Joint Report is available in Spanish, one of the best of which appears to be in the Primary Source Edition (facsimile edition) of *Historia General Y Natural De Las Indias: Islas Y Tierrafirme Del Mar Oceano,* published in Spain in 1853. It was much more difficult to find English translations of the Joint Report. Portions of the Joint Report appear to have been first translated into English by Buckingham Smith in *Historical Magazine,* Vol. XII, in December 1867, although a copy has not been located in undertaking this research. The Joint Report is believed to have first been translated to English in its entirety by Harbert Davenport. It was published in *The Southwestern Historical Quarterly,* Volume 27, in 1924. No book could be found with a title indicating that it contained an English translation of the Joint Report. I found an obscure and very small paperpack published in Albuquerque in 1977, entitled *The Expedition of Pánfilo de Narváez,* by Gerald Theissen, expecting to find that it contained yet another translation of the *Relación.* I was pleasantly surprised to find that it was actually a translation of the Joint Report with a notation that it had been reprinted with the permission of the Imprint Society. Further reseach found that the Imprint Society had published, in 1972, *The Narrative of Cabeza de Vaca*, containing Fanny Bandelier's translation of the *Relación*, and that it contained in the same book, "Oviedo's Version of the Joint Report, presented to the Audiencia in Santo Domingo" translated by Gerald Theissen. Gerald Theisen was a professor of history at the University of Albuquerque who had written a number of books on the subject of the early Spanish exploration of New Mexico and the southwest. He had obviously written his translation for the Imprint Society and later been given permission to print his small paperback as a separate publication.

APPENDIX II

Determining Latitude in the Early Sixteenth Century

Although the *Relación* does not mention latitudes, they were certainly known and used by his pilots and critical for determining the locations of ports and their approximate ships' location while at sea. For more than one thousand years, astronomers had used patterns of stars in the sky, called by different names, to identify the guiding stars that they sought. The sun, moon, and other planets were used, but the most reliable was the North Star, as it stays close to a fixed place in the sky and can be seen almost anywhere in the Northern Hemisphere. What we call the North Star is forty-six times larger than our sun, 2.4 quadrillion miles away, and is situated almost directly over the north pole. Contrary to popular belief, the North Star (Polaris) is only a moderately bright star, ranking forty-eighth in lists of the brightest stars, and can be hard to find. Observers find the North Star by using a pattern of seven stars that we now call the "Big Dipper" within the constellation of Ursa Major (The Great Bear). Two stars in the Big Dipper, the "pointer stars" in the bowl of the Big Dipper, point toward the North Star in Ursa Minor (The Little Bear).

There was a significant evolution in the accuracy in the determination of latitudes from the late fifteenth century to the second and third decades of the sixteenth century. This was achieved primarily by the formation of the *Casa de Contratación* in Seville in 1503 and the creation of a center for accumulation of information relating to piloting and navigation when a pilot-major was appointed in 1508. The appointment of a pilot-major was the beginning a formal process to produce instruments, train pilots in their use, and produce maps and navigational information for the use of those traveling to the New World.

The earliest latitudes reported prior to the centralized training that took place at the *Casa de Contratación* were often wildly inaccurate. There are numerous examples of incorrect latitudes recorded by early explorers, particularly those of Christopher Columbus. He had determined his latitude in the Bahamas to be 42°N, the approximate latitude of Massachusetts.

By the late 1400s, if not earlier, the cosmographers at Seville had determined that Polaris moved the least of all of the stars in the heavens, in a small circle of about 3 ½° in radius. Peter Martyr of Anghiera wrote, in a letter to Cardinal Ludovico in 1499:

> It is well known, illustrious Prince, that the pole star, which our sailors call Tramontana, is not the pole's rotating point of the axis of the heavens. That is easily realized if one looked at the same star through a small opening at its first rising and then again later, through the same opening but in the last part of the night, when dawn puts the stars to flight; at this point one realizes that the star has moved.

In 1500, the radius of Polaris's circle that circumscribed true north was 3 ½°. A sighting of the North Star, absent a necessary correction, could produce a latitude estimate that was 3 ½° too far north or south, depending on the time of night that it was taken. (Today, the radius of the circle is only 7/10 of one degree). In order to find the center point, True North, they had to first sight Polaris, measure its height in degrees, and then apply a correction based on a correction table, or on the relationship of the North Star to other stars, known as the "guards of the Little Bear" as contained in "The Rules of the North Star." It is possible that early pilots either did not know of, or wrongly applied, the Rule of the North Star necessary to determine True North, resulting in recorded latitudes being inconsistent and varying by as much as 3 ½°, even if their navigational instruments were properly employed.

In order to determine their latitude, pilots used the cross-staff, astrolabe, or quadrant. The cross-staff was basically a long hardwood staff with a shorter sliding crosspiece that could be slid along the staff. By lining up the longer staff with the horizon and then sliding the crosspiece to line up with the sun or North Star, the sliding crosspiece would be at a point on which the angle of degrees are etched, and from that, latitude could be determined. It was relatively easy to use but required simultaneous sighting of both the horizon and the sun or North Star. The astrolabe and quadrant did not require sighting the horizon, as they used gravity to keep the instrument aligned vertically. In using the astrolabe, the pilot suspended it with one arm or hung it from a post or tree branch, lining up the sun or the North Star with a guide on the instrument, usually two pinholes through which the sun or North Star was sighted. The angle of declination of the sun at noon, or North Star at night, was etched on the instrument. This angle as adjusted by the Rule of the North Star, or from solar declination tables, allowed latitude to be determined. The preferred instrument for determining latitude was the quadrant. The quadrant was basically a protractor with a weighted line (a plumb bob) attached to its apex. By sighting the sun or North Star though two small aligned pinholes, the plumb bob would cause the line to cross at a point at which the degrees were etched. The angle in degrees was used to measure the degrees of Polaris over the horizon, or the sun at noon, which was then corrected to establish latitude using tables in the *espejo* or the Rules of the North Star.

A quadrant was an instrument created to represent one-fourth of a circle (thus its name) from a point directly above the pilot to the horizon. The logical way to draw a circle, and to show its degrees, is to place 0° at the apex, as is done with compasses. The degrees would then be shown clockwise, with 90° at three o'clock, 180° at six o'clock, and 270° at nine o'clock. Using such an instrument, the horizon would be at 90° degrees. A more efficient quadrant for determining latitude (the height of the north star over the horizon) would have 90° at its apex and 0° at the horizon. There were, in the late 1400s and early 1500s, two variations of the astrolabe produced, one with 0° at the apex and 90° at the horizon, and another with 90° at the apex and 0° at the horizon. If using a quadrant with 0° at the apex, the horizon would be 90°. It may be that some early pilots used such a quadrant. For mariners determining their latitude, a quadrant with 90° at the apex would produce, for example, a correct latitude for Tampa Bay of 28°N. The quadrant with 0° at the apex would produce a wildly incorrect latitude of 62°N (somewhere just south of the Arctic Circle) if not corrected by subtracting the degrees etched on the scale from 90°. It may be that before formal training and controlled manufacture of nautical instruments were consolidated at the *Casa de Contratación*, untrained pilots using incorrectly calibrated instruments produced some of the incorrect latitudes recorded by the earliest expeditionaries.

To determine latitude, the pilot must determine the degrees of the North Star over the horizon, or the declination of the sun from directly overhead at noon. The Tropic of Cancer is the latitude in the Northern Hemisphere at which the sun is directly overhead at noon on June 21, the summer solstice. The Tropic of Cancer line is shown on the Ribero and Colón maps to be at 23.5°N. It is determined by modern technology to be at 23.44°N. Declination tables allow the determination of latitude when the sun is not directly overhead at noon. When Polaris is used, the degrees of the star over the horizon, when corrected by the Rule of the Norh Star, determines latitude.

Latitudes that pilots recorded after the *Casa de Contratación* began a disciplined program for certifying nautical instruments and training pilots in their use became considerably more accurate. Latitudes reported and recorded after 1508 (the year a pilot-major was first appointed at the *Casa de Contratación*) became increasingly more correct, and by the mid-1520s, were generally within a degree (seventy miles) or less of the precise positions determined by using technology of today. The progression in the ability to establish correct latitudes can be found by comparing those recorded before the *Casa de Contratración* established rigid training requirements for pilots sailing to the Indies with those recorded in later years. The latitude of Seville was reported in 1499 by Peter Martyr of Anghiera to be 36°. Using GPS, we know it to be 37.4°. Martyr also wrote, "Madeira, as sailors report, is at 32°." The actual GPS latitude of Funchal, Madeira, is 32.6°.

In Jerald Milanich's *Charting Juan Poncé de León's 1513 Voyage to Florida*, he wrote that Ponce de León's pilot recorded that "the Martires [Keys] are at 26.15 degrees." The actual midpoint of the Keys is 25.26°. Milanich identified a consistent error of one and a half degrees too far north in virtually all of the latitudes recorded by Ponce de León's pilot. It is possible that Ponce de León's pilot, choosing to do his sightings at a particular time each night, would have a consistent error on every latitude recorded if he had not done the necessary correction by applying the Rule of the North Star.

Latitudes indicated on the 1527 Colón and 1529 Ribero maps, and in the Chavez *espejo* of the late 1530s, demonstrate how much the pilots had improved in their determination of latitudes as the result of their training at the *Casa de Contratación*. In a study done by Joaquim Alves Gaspar, he determined that on the earliest charts he examined, those of Juan de la Cosa in 1500, the largest latitude error found was 12°. By 1519 on the Kunstman IV chart, it had reduced to 3°, and in the latest chart he examined, the Salviati Planisphere of c. 1525, the largest error found was 2°. Based on the comparison of GPS with those shown on the Chavez *espejo* of the 1530s, and as shown on maps produced in 1527 and 1529 examined elsewhere in this book, the latitudes, with few exceptions, are within 2/10 to 3/10 of one degree (fourteen to twenty-one miles) of their actual locations.

In spite of the accuracy of the determination of latitude by sightings taken from land, sailors had to establish their latitudes at sea on moving ships. These rough latitude estimates were used more to determine general directional aiming points than as precise indicators of a ship's position. One degree of latitude was approximately seventy miles. Once an approximation of latitude had been determined at sea, the pilots could be reasonably confident that they could establish their direction to a coastal port within seventy to one hundred miles of its actual location and then use visible landmarks to find the port they sought. It was a practice of the day to intentionally aim at a latitude that was well south or well north of the intended destination, referred to as "running down the latitude" so that when land was first seen, the pilots would know which direction to travel along the coast to find the port that they sought.

The West-Central Florida Coastline in 1500: How the Explorers Saw It.

Ping Wang, PhD
Professor, School of Geosciences
University of South Florida

The following is a simplified and supplemental overview of a detailed presentation at The History Council Symposium in St. Petersburg, FL, on October 27, 2018. Additional detail is available from the author
at pwang@usf.edu

The purpose of this study was to determine the general characteristics of the west-central Florida coastline five hundred years ago during "the age of exploration" and to analyze bays and harbors that would have existed at the time, with the purpose of identifying bay entrances and landing sites that would have been navigable by ships of the era with drafts of ten to fourteen feet.

General Characteristics of the West-Central Florida Coastline c. 1500

When the last Ice Age ended due to global warming, starting approximately eighteen thousand years ago, the sea levels began to rise. For the next fourteen thousand years, sea levels rose very rapidly by an estimated 400 feet, or at 0.4 inches per year. The impact of this rise in sea levels was the reduction of the area of the Florida Peninsula by approximately 60 percent, submerging vast areas of the present-day continental shelf, which, prior to that, were dry land. At about six thousand to eight thousand years ago, the rate of sea-level rise slowed down substantially to about 0.1 inches per year. Starting at about that time, present-day Tampa Bay and Charlotte Harbor were flooded by seawater and became the estuaries that we see today.

Sea level at the west-central Florida coastline reached close to its present position approximately two thousand to four thousand years ago. The rate of sea-level rise slowed further down at that time to about 0.04 inches per year. At that time, the chain of barrier islands started to develop along the coast. Radiocarbon dating and archaeological discoveries have indicated that many existing barrier islands have been in their present location for more than one thousand years. The absence of radiocarbon dating or archaeological discoveries on other barrier islands simply indicates the lack of data and does not prove that they were not there. It is also known that some barrier islands have been formed, or have shrunken or disappeared, during the past five centuries. An example, Egmont Key, illustrates the point. While archaeological evidence proves that Egmont Key has existed for an estimated two thousand years, it is known that in the mid-1800s it was nearly twice as wide as it is today. Whether it was smaller or larger in 1500 is unknown, but it demonstrates that barrier islands, while always being present on the coastline, have been subject to considerable change as to size, location, and even existence during the past five centuries.

Large scale coastal morphology changes are caused by sea-level rise or fall, in addition to sediment deposited from rivers or from seaward from the continental shelf. In the case of the west-central Florida coast, sea level did not change significantly over the past five hundred years. Furthermore, rivers in Florida do not carry large amounts of sediment to the coast and are not capable of causing large scale morphology change in a short geological time. Sediment supply from the continental shelf is controlled by rate of sea-level change. The relatively slow sea-level rise over the past five hundred years would not have induced large onshore sediment movement and subsequent regional scale morphology change. Therefore, no major morphology changes have occurred during the past five hundred years. The coast in 1500 CE was generally similar to that of today's, with the exception of the impact of substantial alterations by humans in some areas, primarily dredging of channels, landfill, and construction of causeways and bridges during the past one hundred years.

In a broad sense, the west-central coastline of Florida during the past one thousand years has not undergone significant change. It consists of two headlands, Indian Rocks Beach in Pinellas County and Sanibel Island, south of Charlotte Harbor; and two large estuaries, Tampa Bay and Charlotte Harbor, as well as a significant number of smaller bays along the coastline, all bordered seaward by a chain of barrier islands punctuated by numerous tidal inlets.

The west-central Florida coast has a wide, gentle, and shallow inner continental shelf. Based on an 1870s bathymetry map, the six-meter (twenty-foot) contour (relative to Mean Sea Level) is located at about four to six miles from the shoreline, or almost at the limit that one could see the land from a ship offshore. The four-meter (thirteen-foot) contour is located at 0.5 to 1.5 miles from the shoreline. It is worth noting that the thirteen-foot contour, i.e., about eleven feet at spring low tide, may have been too shallow for the vessels, requiring ships to stay at least ½ to 1 ½ miles offshore in order to stay safely in deeper waters while attempting to identify bay or harbor entrances.

The two largest harbors on the west Florida coastline, Charlotte Harbor and Tampa Bay, have been mostly unchanged during the past several millennia. Other smaller estuaries, including Boca Ciega Bay, Sarasota Bay, Lemon Bay, and Estero Bay, were in approximately their present locations in 1500 CE.

The coastal geology of west Florida contains no hills, mountains, or promontories that would be available as landmarks from which early pilots/navigators could have determined their location. The coastline is generally flat and is made up of barrier islands and coastline with no remarkable features from which to deduce location. However, the Pinellas Headland at Indian Rocks Beach protrudes nearly seven miles into the Gulf of Mexico, relative to the main entrance to Tampa Bay. It is possible that the early sailors who were sailing northward along the coast, e.g., along the twenty-foot contour, four to six miles offshore, might have recognized this protruding headland as a landmark.

Many storms and hurricanes have impacted the west-central Florida coast during the past five centuries. Although the hurricanes do not have the ability to fundamentally alter the general coastal landscape, they can substantially alter the localized configurations of the barrier island chain, particularly in terms of tidal inlet locations. This is discussed in more detail in the following concerning the specific bays and harbors. It is worth specifying here that hurricanes would not have been able to cause dramatic changes at the main Egmont Channel entrances to Tampa Bay or to the Boca Grande Inlet at Charlotte Harbor.

In summary: the west-central Florida coastline of 1500 CE was remarkably similar in the depth of water, presence of barrier islands, and locations of bays and harbors to the coastline of today.

Characteristics of Specific Bays and Harbors

Although the smaller bays (Boca Ciega Bay, Sarasota Bay, Lemon Bay, and Estero Bay) are in the same general locations, the locations of tidal inlets into these bays could have been in different locations than those of today. Storms and hurricanes could open up a new inlet and cause an old inlet to close. Such a process typically takes a few decades. An example is the opening of John's Pass in 1848 by a hurricane, which caused a subsequent rapid southward migration, of up to five hundred feet per year, of Blind Pass. If Blind Pass had not been stabilized by human engineering, it would have likely closed.

Before John's Pass was opened in 1848, Blind Pass would have been the main inlet into Boca Ciega Bay. The size of Boca Ciega Bay requires that it has an outlet connecting to the Gulf of Mexico. The size of the pass, prior to the opening of John's Pass in 1848, would roughly be the sum of today's John's Pass and Blind Pass. Based on the characteristics of many similar inlets along the west-central Florida coast, the main channel between the two barrier islands would be wide and deep enough for vessels with drafts of ten to fifteen feet to sail through. However, like almost all other inlets, with the exception of the main entrance to Tampa Bay, the challenge for the early sailors would be to pass through the shallower water at the seaward edge of the pass (technically referred to as the terminal lobe) and to find anchorage with deep water landward of the inlet. Based on the present morphologies of the ebb and flood shoals at the unstructured inlets along the west-central Florida coast, getting past the shallow terminal lobe would be very difficult at some inlets and virtually impossible at others.

A key element in determining the size of an inlet is the volume of water that flows landward (flood tide) into the bay and seaward (ebb tide) into the Gulf through the inlet. This volume of tidal water, referred to as the tidal prism, and the additional water from rivers (if any), and the number of inlets for water to flow through during incoming and outgoing tides, controls the width and depth of the channel/s that would be required to maintain the regular exchange of seawater between the bay and the Gulf. Several empirical equations have been developed, linking the tidal prism to the size of the cross-section of the inlet. A commonly used relationship between tidal prism (P) during a spring tide and minimum equilibrium inlet cross-sectional area (Ac) for the Gulf coast inlets is as follows:

$$A_c = 9.311 \times 10^{-4} \, P^{0.84} \text{ (Using metric units)}$$

This formula can be used to estimate the cross-sectional area of inlet/s serving a particular bay. Using Boca Ciega Bay as an example, with data based on historical charts, the area of the bay was approximately twenty-six million square meters before the human alterations. The average spring tidal range in this area is 1.05 meters. This yields a tidal prism of roughly twenty-seven million cubic meters. Based on the above formula, the equilibrium minimum cross-sectional area of the inlet serving the Boca Ciega Bay is about 1,600 square meters, or roughly 17,000 square feet. West-central Florida tidal inlets, such as today's John's Pass and Bunces Pass, have a depth of sixteen to eighteen feet. This would give a width of Boca Ciega Bay inlet of about one thousand feet. It is worth noting that the above calculation yields the cross-sectional area typically between the two barrier islands. It does not predict the cross-sectional areas (depth of water) of the seaward end or the landward end of the inlet.

For purposes of this analysis, we have used Mean Sea Level (MSL) to estimate water depths. MSL is the midpoint between high and low tides. In general, there are two high tides and two low tides each day on the west Florida coast. The maximum spring tide ranges from nearly two feet above MSL to two feet below MSL. The maximum spring tidal range is therefore roughly four feet from the highest to the lowest tide. Using MSL as a baseline, we can add two feet to estimate channel and bay depths at maximum spring high tide. However, ships entering or leaving a harbor would most likely use the incoming or outgoing tide to assist them, which would require entering a harbor on an incoming (still rising) tide, or leaving a harbor on an outgoing (water depth decreasing) tide. It is thus reasonable to assume that determining the navigability of bay or harbor openings should be based on MSL.

Historians have postulated that early explorers may have entered and anchored in Old Tampa Bay, Tampa Bay proper, Sarasota Bay, Boca Ciega Bay, Charlotte Harbor, Lemon Bay, and Estero Bay. These bays were studied in an effort to determine whether navigable entry and anchorages could have existed in these places, and to identify any other bays or harbors that have the characteristics that would allow a vessel drawing ten to fourteen feet to enter and anchor.

Charlotte Harbor has three rather large rivers, Peace and Myakka Rivers to the north and Calusahatchee River to the south. The relatively large amounts of sediment (sand and mud) brought into the bay by these rivers are responsible for the overall shallow water in Charlotte Harbor and the complicated shoal features within the bay. In contrast, Tampa Bay receives no major river, except the much smaller Manatee River near its entrance. The overall deeper Tampa Bay, without complicated shoal features, resulted from the lack of sediment input from rivers. The different bathymetric characteristics of Tampa Bay and Charlotte Harbor can be explained by their geology.

A review of the general morphology, as well as tidal prisms and tidal flow patterns of Tampa Bay, Charlotte Harbor, Sarasota Bay, Boca Ciega Bay, Lemon Bay, and Estero Bay, reveals the following:

1. Tampa Bay—Tampa Bay has two wide and deep entrances on either side of Egmont key. They are easily sufficient to support a ship drawing ten to fifteen feet. Water depths would allow such ships to sail into and through the full length of Tampa Bay. Many sites for suitable anchorages exist.

2. Old Tampa Bay—Entry into Old Tampa Bay was possible, as the entrance channel would have been sufficiently deep. There are several areas inside Old Tampa Bay that could support anchorage.

3. Charlotte Harbor—The main entrance, Boca Grande Inlet, could have supported large ships entering the bay, although the depth of approaches to this channel would make it more challenging than Tampa Bay due to the large and mostly shallow ebb shoal. There are areas directly landward of Boca Grande inlet that possibly could support anchorage, but it is safe to say that going over that outer shoal

(we call it the terminal lobe over an ebb tidal delta) would not really have been possible by large ships in the 1500s.

4.   Boca Ciega Bay and Estero Bay—These two small bays provide similar conditions as discussed above concerning Boca Ciega Bay. The inlets serving these bays likely had one main channel for each bay that was deep and wide enough for vessels drawing ten to fifteen feet. The major challenges for the early sailors would be to navigate over the shallower terminal lobe in order to reach the deeper channel and to find deep water inside the bay for anchorage. The bathymetry map from the 1870s shows narrow entrances into the channels and small areas within the bays that are deep enough for anchoring. However, it is not clear if the early sailors had the precision to navigate these waters.

5.   Lemon Bay and Sarasota Bay—Neither of these bays appear to have been navigable by deep-draft ships in 1500 CE. In the case of Lemon Bay, the tidal prism would not have produced channels of the required depth. In the case of Sarasota Bay, there were three inlets serving

the bay, which would result in shallower inlets. In addition, the shallow bedrock level in Sarasota Bay would result in practically no area deep enough for anchoring.

6. A maximum speed of tidal driven flow is about three to four feet, or about two knots. This current velocity should be expected for most of the inlets. It is often referred to as an equilibrium velocity, in that if the flow is stronger, it would scour the channel and make it larger and subsequently result in a slower flow, and vice versa. This two-knot water speed would have been a significant factor in aiding or hindering ships as they attempted to enter or leave through a pass.

In summary, in terms of bays that would be considered the most-likely prospects for early navigators to enter, anchor and exit, Tampa Bay presents the least difficult choice to the mariner, and perhaps the easiest to find. Tampa Bay is just below the Pinellas Headlands, extending seven miles to the west from the coast. As the most-westward headland visible to seafarers as they sailed north along the coast of Florida, it may have represented a significant landmark and a point from which to deduce the location of Tampa Bay. (Boca

Ciega Bay is just south of this headland, just north of the Tampa Bay entrance.)

Charlotte Harbor also represents a possible point of entry and anchorage. It has a deep main channel and in places has sufficient depth inside the main channel for possible anchorage. It has more entry/exit channels and a smaller tidal prism, resulting in shallower channels and shallower approaches to the main and deepest channel, Boca Grande Pass. It is very unlikely that ships with drafts of ten or more feet could have successfully reached the pass or anchored within the bay due to the ebb shoals at its entrance and shallow depth within.

Both Estero Bay and Boca Ciega Bay would have had channels sufficient for large ships of the 1500s, but the shallows approaching the main channels, and the depths of the bays themselves, would likely have prevented them from entering.

Neither Lemon Bay nor Sarasota Bay appear to have the characteristics that would have provided channels with sufficient water depth, or depth within the bay, to support large ships of the era.

Bathymetric charts for Tampa Bay and Old Tampa Bay derived from mid-1800s data are available at pwang@usf.edu.

APPENDIX IV

Analysis of the Colón and 1529 Ribero Map Differences

No detailed study of legends and toponyms contained on the various maps was undertaken, but several similarities and differences became immediately apparent:

1. Structure: When placed side by side, the margins of the maps, the latitude scales, and the lines drawn for the Tropic of Cancer, Equator, Tropic of Capricorn, and Papal Line are identical.

2. Haiti: The island of Hispaniola is identified as such on the 1527 Colón/Kohl map. It is identified as Haiti on the Ribero maps.

3. The Shape of Florida: The Colón map much more accurately displays the true shape of Florida than the Ribero maps.

4. <u>The Shape of the Gulf of Mexico</u>: The shape of the Gulf of Mexico is significantly elongated, east/west, on the Colón map. It is closer to its actual shape on the 1529 Ribero maps. This demonstrates the difficulty encountered by pilots and mapmakers who had no reliable method of determining longitude. The determination of the width of the Gulf had been based on distances between known landmarks on the northern Gulf coast and/or distance traveled in sailing across the Gulf.

5. <u>Latitudes indicated on maps</u>: An analysis of latitudes indicated on the maps resulted in a determination that the latitudes on the Colón and Ribero maps are generally accurate and closely conform with each other, but the Ribero maps are about one degree "off," to the south, on the Florida coast. The toponym nearest a river opening or bay drawn on the map was chosen as the point from which to measure latitude. Variances of two- or three-tenths of degrees may be attributable to an incorrect selection of a place on the map associated with a particular toponym.

6. <u>The Shape of the Yucatán</u>: As is the case with the shape of the Gulf of Mexico, the Colón maps do not approximate the true shape of the Yucatán. The USLC Colón map differs from the Colón/Kohl map in that the Yucatán appears as an island on the Kohl but has been connected to the mainland in the USLC version, indicating that whoever traced the Kohl map had corrected it to show that the Yucatán was not an island. There also appears to be a subtle difference in the shape of the Yucatán between the two Ribero maps. Since they are believed to be two variations of the same map, this may be an indicator that one was produced with later information than the other.

7. <u>Bahia Honda</u>: No *"Bahia Honda"* appears on either the Colón or Ribero maps

8. <u>Handwriting</u>: All but the Ribero/Propaganda map are copies of the original. Analysis of handwriting on the maps does not enable a determination of its original producer.

9. <u>Spelling and Nomenclature</u>: There is no consistency in the spelling or in the

nomenclature on the maps. For example, Brazil is identified as:

- Tera de Brasilis on the Ribero/Propaganda map
- Tiera del Brasil on the Ribero/Kohl map
- EL BRASIL on the Colón/Kohl map

10. <u>Legends and toponyms</u>: The Propaganda map has twelve lengthy descriptive legends that are absent on the Colón maps. The maps are very similar in legends and cartouches in many cases, but there are some obvious and significant differences. An example is in the legends relating to Ayllón on the Ribero maps.

- On the Ribero map presented in Kohl, the legend reads: "Land of Ayllón which he discovered and returned to settle because it is land well-disposed to produce bread (wheat) and wine and all things from Spain: died here from disease."

- On the Propaganda map, the legend is, "Here went the licentiate Ayllón to settle the country for which he sailed from S. Domingo, or Puerto de Plata, where his men were taken on board. They took with them very little provisions, and the natives fled into the interior from fear. So that when winter set in many of them died of cold and hunger . . . they determined to return to Hispaniola."

It appears that the Kohl version was written earlier than the Propaganda version, as the first part of the description is forward-looking with high expectations, as if it were written after Ayllón left but before news of his death was known, followed by a few words added after news of his death reached Spain, probably in late 1526 or very early in 1527. The Propaganda version was clearly written in its entirety after the failure of the Ayllón settlement had become known in Spain.

11. Dating the Maps: The dates on the maps do not represent the geographic and topographic knowledge available at the *Casa de Contratación* at the time of their completion dates or the date that they are presumed to have been created. The legends and toponyms on the "1529" maps clearly predate those on the 1527 maps. While the Ribero/Propaganda and Ribero/Kohl maps are generally believed

to be two versions of the same map, and a brief analysis supports that premise, closer inspection reveals some differences that could indicate that one was produced slightly earlier than the other. The difference in the identification of Brasil, the shape of the Yucatán, and differences in references to Magellan suggest that the toponyms and legends they contain must be examined minutely by historians and cartographers to determine if they are two versions of the same map (as is generally believed) or if there are meaningful differences in legends and/ or toponyms, perhaps establishing that one might have been drawn with information gained later than the other.

12. Illustrations and Cartouches: The maps present a fascinating array of navigational information and sailing directions, presented in cartouches or illustrations.

Ship illustrations: While at first glance the ships appearing on the maps appear to be merely artistic enhancements, they are actually intended to show the sailing routes to be followed. Magnification of the Ribero/

Kohl map shows a ship headed toward the Indies and below it an inscription: *"boy a las Indias"* (going to the Indies), and two ships in the Indies, one headed northeast and another west, have a subscript, *"bengo de las Indias"* (coming from the Indies).

Cartouches: There are highly detailed drawings of nautical instruments accompanied by cartouches with very specific instructions as to their proper use to make solar and star sightings, and how to use conversion tables.

APPENDIX V
Analysis of the "Propaganda" Map Chigi Attribution

The Propaganda map contains one escutcheon and two coats of arms at the base of the map. It is not possible to reproduce the portion of the map displaying the coats of arms, as they are too far apart, and reduction in scale would make them impossible to see. An excellent 1529 Ribero "Propaganda" map showing the coats of arms and escutcheons can be seen online, thanks to the Norman Leventhal Map and Education Center at the Boston Public Library. The map had been digitized and can be downloaded. Their website is found at collections.leventhalmap.org. Clearer versions of the escutcheon and coats of arms are seen below:

Combined Chigi/Della Rovere

Escutcheon of Pope Julius II

Chigi Coat of Arms

The escutcheon at the center at the base of the map is that of Pope Julius II, who had approved the Treaty of Tordesillas in a Papal Bull on January 1506. The title of the map refers to the treaty of Tordesillas, saying that it is "divided in two parts according to the agreement made by the Catholic Majesties of Spain and King John of Portugal at Tordesillas, A.D. 1494." Pope Julius's papal escutcheon (center) includes his Della Rovere family coat of arms. The coat of arms to the right are those of the Chigi family. To the left are the combined Chigi/Della Rovere coats of arms.

Lorenzo Leone Chigi was, in 1529, at the age of 22, the richest man in Rome. His father, Agostino Chigi, "il Magnifico," had died in 1520. Agostino had been a close ally of Pope Julius II, banker to the church, and said to be the richest banker in the world. Pope Julius II had given Agostino Chigi the privilege of quartering the Chigi family coat of arms with that of his own.

The Propaganda *Carta Universal* was probably commissioned from Diego Ribero by Lorenzo Chigi in 1529, perhaps as a gift to Pope Clement VII, thus gaining its place in the Papal library in Rome. It may be the greatly enhanced *Padrón Real,* which had been rendered obsolete in 1526 when Carlos I ordered a new *Padrón General* to be created. The artistic enhancement of the Propaganda map resulted in what has been called the most beautiful map created by the mapmakers in Seville. The subsequent 1527 "Colon" map may be the first *Padrón General*.

Kohl's *General-Karten von Amerika* and Florida toponym translations

Johann Georg Kohl published in 1860 *Die Beiden Ältesten General-Karten von Amerika Ausgeführt in den Jahren 1527 und 1529*. He was a brilliant scholar and author of twenty-five books, ranging in subjects from the development of transportation and characteristics of cities of the future to a history of the Gulf Stream. He was known as an accomplished mapmaker and historian. By 1860 he had become very prominent as a scientist and historian, and included among his acquaintances were Henry Wadsworth Longfellow, Washington Irving, and Ralph Waldo Emerson. Though sometimes referred to as "Doctor" Kohl, the title is apparently an honorific, as his studies of law had been interrupted at a young age. His prominence as a researcher, historian, and author gave him access to study and make copies of the originals of the 1527 and

1529 *cartas universales* at the Grand-Ducal Library in Weimar. He began his book after his visit to the United States from 1854–1858. As was his wont, he studied the maps in minute detail and used his research skills to write a book of 160,000 words to accompany the maps, which were copied in remarkable detail.

The number of copies of *Die Beiden Ältesten* that were printed, and the total number remaining, is unknown. There are currently twenty-three copies in libraries in the United States and twenty-five are in libraries in Europe. The number that may be in private collections is unknown. The author's copy of this book was acquired in March 2020. It contains a label acknowledging that the book was originally gifted to the American Geographical Society (AGS) in 1876 by Walton W. Evans of New York. Written by hand on the inside front cover is "Duplicate," indicating that the AGS apparently disposed of it sometime after 1876. At the time of this writing, there are no other copies of this book for sale anywhere in the world. The book has not been translated into English, reprinted, or republished, and full-scale copies of the maps that it contains have apparently never been produced.

Not bound in, but included separately with the book, are two folded maps. They are copies of the 1527 and 1529 *Cartas Universales*, taken from the originals in the

Grand-Ducal Library in Weimar, Germany. Each map is 27" x 36" when opened.

It is relatively commonplace to find that maps in rare books have been removed for framing and the book discarded. That may explain the extreme rarity of the book and suggests that some of these maps may have been framed, thus losing the context of their origination and resulting in their not being recognized for their extreme importance to history and cartography.

Although the U.S. Library of Congress has a copy, it is unlikely that previous researchers have had the opportunity to access the book or the freedom to remove, open, and copy the maps that it contains. The size of the maps prevents them from being scanned by most printers or scanners.

It is very likely that the only previous students of these maps were cartographers who did not closely study the many hundreds of legends and toponyms that the maps contain. It appears from their written descriptions that many of the cartographers who wrote about these maps had never actually seen them. Those who appear to have seen the maps chose only selected portions of the map to describe. Unless one had a particular interest in *La Florida* (with the exception of Kohl, none of the cartographers who wrote about the "Weimar" maps apparently had), little notice would be made of an area of two square inches on a 972-square-inch map.

Kohl, in his 160,000-word book, provides extensive details concerning the originals from which his maps were copied, and highly detailed analyses of most legends, cartouches, and toponyms. The book has not been translated into English, although I copied the appropriate pages from the book (pp. 73–74) and obtained an English translation of Kohl's references to toponyms on Florida's west coast:

> *R de la Paz. The map from 1527 has at about 26°N a R de la Paz (River of Peace), which is missing from Ribero. This river and name must also be rooted in the Ponce de León expedition. The name still appears on many maps of the sixteenth century in this area. So, for example, the work of de Moyne published by De Bry in 1595, who joined Ribault's expedition in 1562. [Theil took part?] under the name "Flumen Pacis." It can still be found on countless other maps, including those from the seventeenth century. Mr. Buckingham Smith has suggested that an English geographer translated this name to "Peace River" and, corrupting "Pease" or "Pea River" (the Pea River), has become what name of a river that leads today to our Charlotte Bay or Carlos Bay.*

<u>R de Canoas.</u> *Our two charts have the name R de Canoas. It is a name that the Spaniards often gave to rivers, from the mouths of which they saw curious Indians driving their canoes when they appeared. Perhaps this name denotes the place where Ponce ships first raised the alarm among the Indians in the year and where Spaniards and Floridians first saw each other. The name is repeated on later charts, e.g. B. at Vaz Dourado (1580). Even today we still have a "canoe river" on the west coast of Florida, but not quite as wide.*

<u>B. de Jua Ponce on 1529; B. de Juhan Ponce on 1527.</u> *After Ponce de León had sailed around the south coast and the chain of the Martyr rocks, he entered the Gulf of Mexico on May 16 and cruised north and northeast. On May 24, he saw land again and dropped anchor at some small islands that lay deep in a bay. There he looked for a Cacique Carlos he had heard of and who was said to be rich in gold, and had various peaceful and hostile transactions with the natives until June 3, where he sailed again. About the location of these transactions and the position of the big beautiful ones, Bay des Cacique Carlos, that Ponce discovered, and which soon appears to be called "La Bahia de Juan Ponce" and*

"Bahia de Cacique Carlos" in Spain, we have had different opinions. The usual opinion has opted for the southernmost of the three large bays, which stands at 25 ½°, it is very wide but not deep, and is unsuitable for anchoring.

The next big bay to the north is our current Charlotte Harbor or S. Carlos Bay, which stands at about 26° 50. It was previously thought to be the actual Ponce Bay, namely by Herrera, who describes it precisely in his description of West India, distinguishing it from the more northern Tampa Bay, and says it is called "the Bay of Carlos or Juan Ponce." Our map of Ribero also seems to explain this view. It has a deep bay at 26 ½°, which looks a bit like today's Charlotte Bay, and calls it "B. de Juan Ponce."

One degree north of Charlotte Bay is the third major bay on the west coast of Florida and the most significant, deep, and navigable of all, the famous Tampa Bay. I do not know whether this was also a significant geographical anchorage for Ponce, but our map from 1527 seems to indicate that it is. I already noticed above that the configuration of Florida is better than that of the 1529 map. The peninsula has just the right proportions on it. This map from 1527, which is so good in the parts concerned, now includes the name "Bahia de Juan Ponce" as the northernmost of the bays mentioned, which, like our Tampa Bay, is at 28°N, and is supposed to represent this bay.

Bibliography

Adorno, Rolena and Patrick Charles Pautz. *Álvar Núñez Cabeza de Vaca: His Account, His Life, and the Expedition of Pánfilo de Narváez*. 3 Vols. Lincoln and London: University of Nebraska Press, 1999 [See also Núñez Cabeza de Vaca, Álvar for their one-volume annotated translation of the *Relación*].

Anghiera, Peter Martyr d'. *The Discovery of the New World in the Writings of Peter Martyr of Anghiera*. Edited and translated by The Ohio State University. Rome: Instituto Poligrafico e Zecca Dello Stato. Libreria dello Stato. 1992.

———. *De Orbe Novo, Volume I (of 2)—The Eight Decades of Peter Martyr D'Anghera*. Translated from the Latin by Francis Augustus MacNutt. 1912. (Filiquarian Publishing. Coppell, TX. 2019.)

Baldacci, Osvaldo. *Columbian Atlas of the Great Discovery*. English translation of *Nuova Raccolta Colombiana*. Rome: Instituto Poligrafico E Zecca Dello Stato. Liberia Dello Stato, 1992.

Balsera, Viviana Díaz and Rachel A. May. *La Florida: 500 Years of Hispanic Presence*. Gainesville: University Press of Florida, 2014.

Bandelier, Fanny. *The Narrative of Alvar Núñez Cabeza de Vaca*. Translated and annotated by Fanny Bandelier. [Also contains Thiesen's translation of Oviedo's summary of the

Joint Report]. Barre, Massachusetts: The Imprint Society, 1972.

Barcia Carballido y Zúñiga, Andrés González de. *Barcia's Chronological History of the Continent of Florida.* Translated by Anthony Kerrigan. Gainesville: University of Florida Press, 1951.

———. *Ensayo cronologico, para la Historia General de La Florida.* Madrid, 1722.

Barnett, Captain E. *The West India Pilot.* Volume II. London: Hydrographic Office, Admiralty, 1859.

Beasly, Fred. *First Across North America.* Austin-Dallas: Graphic Ideas, 1974.

Bell, Gregory Jason. "A Caribbean Borderland: The Tampa Bay Area During the Sixteenth Century." USF Scholar Commons, *Tampa Bay History*, Vol. 25 (2011).

Bethell, John A. *History of Pinellas Peninsula.* St. Petersburg: Press of the Independent Job Department, 1914.

Bolton, Herbert Eugene. *Spanish Exploration in the Southwest, 1542–1706.* Primary Source Edition. New York: Barnes & Noble, Inc., 1908.

Burch, David. *Celestial Navigation.* Second Edition. Seattle: Starpath Publications, 2019.

Cabeza de Vaca, Álvar Núñez. (See Núñez Cabeza de Vaca, Álvar).

Casas, Bartolomé de las. *History of the Indies.* Translated and edited by Andrée Collard. New York, Evanston, and London: Harper Torchbooks, 1971.

————. *A Short Account of the Destruction of the Indies.* Edited and translated by Nigel Griffin. London: Penguin Books, 2004.

Casteñeda, Pedro de. *Narrative of the Expedition of Coronado.* Translated by Frederick Hodge in *Spanish Explorers of the Southern United States.* See also Jameson, J Franklin.

Chavez, Alonso de. *Alonso de Chavez y el Libro IV de su Espejo de Navegantes.* Translated and annotated by Paulino Castañeda, Mariano Cuesta, Pilar Hernández. Madrid: Industrias Graficas España, 1977.

————.*Transcripción, estudio y notas del Espejo de Navegantes de Alonso de Chaves.* Translated and annotated by Paulino Castañeda, Mariano Cuesta, Pilar Hernández. Madrid: Instituto de Historia y Cultura Naval, 1983.

Chipman, Donald E. *Álvar Núñez Cabeza de Vaca: The Great Pedestrian of North and South America.* Denton: Texas State Historical Association, 2012.

"In Search of Cabeza de Vaca's Route Across Texas; An Historiographical Survey." *Southwestern Historical Quarterly.* Vol. 91, No. 2. (Oct. 1987: pp. 127–148).

Clayton, Lawrence A., Vernon James Knight, Jr., and Edward C. Moore. *The De Soto Chronicles.* Two Volumes. Tuscaloosa: The University of Alabama Press, 1993.

Coopwood, Bethel. "Notes on the History of La Bahía del Espiritu Santo." *The Quarterly of the Texas State Historical Association.* Vol. 2, No. 2. (Oct. 1898).

Cumming, William P. *The Southeast in Early Maps.* Third Edition. Chapel Hill & London: The University of North Carolina Press, 1998.

Cusick, James G. and Sherry Johnson, Editors. *The Voyages of Ponce de León: Scholarly Perspectives*. Cocoa, FL: The Florida Historical Society Press, 2012.

Daniels, Gary O. "Juan Ortiz Captivity Narrative by Elvas." The NewWorld.us, 2014.

Davies, Sureka. "The Navigational Iconography of Diogo Ribiero's 1529 Vatican Planisphere." *Proceedings of the 19th International Conference on the History of Cartography*. Madrid: July 2001. jstor.org/stable/3594759

Davis, Jack E. *The Gulf: The Making of an American Sea*. New York: Liveright Publishing Corporation, 2017.

Davis, Richard A. *Barrier Islands of the Florida Gulf Coast Peninsula*. Sarasota, FL: Pineapple Press, 2016.

Davis, T. Frederick. "Juan Ponce de Leon's Voyages to Florida." The Quarterly of the Florida Historical Society. Volume XIV, Number 1. Tallahassee, Florida: Office of Publications, July 1935.

Díaz, Bernal. *The Conquest of New Spain*. Translated and introduced by J.M. Cohen. London: The Folio Society, 1974.

Díaz del Castillo, Bernal. *The True History of the Conquest of New Spain*. Indianapolis—Cambridge: Hackett Publishing Company, Inc., 2012.

Dominguez, Luis L. *Chronicles of the Narvaez Expedition*. Digireads.com Book, 2013.

Dunn, Oliver and James E. Kelley, Jr. *The Diario of Christopher Columbus's First Voyage to America 1492-1493*. Norman: University of Oklahoma Press, 1989.

Elvas, Gentleman of. *The Narrative of the Expedition of Hernando de Soto, by the Gentleman of Elvas*. Translated by Buckingham Smith. Bradford Club, 1866. (See Lewis, Theodore. *Spanish Explorers in the Southern United States 1528–1543*. pp. 127–272).

Fisher, Dennis. *Latitude Hooks and Azimuth Rings*. Camden, Maine: International Marine, 1995.

Flint, Richard and Shirley Cushing Flint. *The Coronado Expedition*. Albuquerque: University of New Mexico Press, 2003.

———. *Documents of the Coronado Expedition, 1539–1542*. Dallas: Southern Methodist University Press, 2005.

Folson, George. *The Despatches of Hernando Cortez*. New York: Wiley & Putnam, 1843. Reprinted London: Forgotten Books, 2015.

Fuson, Robert H. *Legendary Islands of the Ocean Sea*. Sarasota, Florida: Pineapple Press, 1995

———. *Juan Ponce de León and the Spanish Discovery of Puerto Rico and Florida*. Blacksburg, VA: The McDonald & Woodward Publishing Company, 2000.

Galloway, Patricia Kay. *The Hernando de Soto Expedition: History, Historiography, and "Discovery" in the Southeast*. Lincoln: University of Nebraska Press, 2006.

Gannon, Michael. *The History of Florida*. Gainesville: University Press of Florida, 1996.

Ganong, W. F. *Crucial Maps in the Early Cartography and Place-Nomenclature of the Atlantic Coast of Canada*. Toronto: University of Toronto Press, 1964.

Garcia, Clotilde P. *Captain Alonso Alvarez de Pineda and the Exploration of the Texas Coast and the Gulf of Mexico*. Austin, Texas: Jenkins Publishing Company, 1982.

Gaspar, Joaquim Alves. Faculty of Science, University Center for Science and Technology, University of Lisbon. Personal Communication.

Goodwin, Robert. *Crossing the Continent 1527–1540.* New York: HarperCollins, 2008.

Grismer, Karl H. *History of St. Petersburg.* St. Petersburg, Florida: The Tourist News Publishing Co, 1924.

Hallenbeck, Cleve. *Álvar Núñez Cabeza de Vaca: The Journey and Route of the First European to Cross the Continent of North America 1534–1536.* Port Washington, New York and London: Kennikat Press, 1940.

Haring, Clarence Henry. *Trade and Navigation Between Spain and the Indies in the Time of the Hapsburgs.* Cambridge: Harvard University Press, 1918.

Harrisse, Henry. *The Discovery of North America (Microform).* [London]: Henry Stevens & Son. MDCCCXCII. (Reproduced from microfilm by Scholar Select).

Henderson, Ann I., and Gary R. Mormino, Eds. *Spanish Pathways in Florida.* Sarasota, FL: Pineapple Press, 1999.

Herrera, [y Tordesillas] Antonio de. *Historia General de los Hechos de los Castellanos en las Islas y Tierra Firme del Mar Oceano.* Madrid: Officina Real de Nicola Rodriguez Franco, 1726.

Herrera y Tordesillas, Antonio de. *The General History of the Vast Continent and Islands of America, Commonly Call'd, the West-Indies, From the First Discovery Therof.* Translated by Capt. John Stevens. Vols I–III. London: Wood and Woodward. MDCCXL. Facsimile edition by Gale ECCO Print. Undated.

————. *The General History of the Vast Continent and Islands of America, Commonly Call'd, the West-Indies, From the First Discovery Therof.* Translated by Capt. John Stevens. Vol. IV. London: Wood and Woodward. MDCCXL. Facsimile edition by Gale ECCO Print. Undated.

Hine, Albert C. *Geologic History of Florida: Major Events That Formed the Sunshine State.* Gainesville: University Press of Florida, 2013.

————. and Don P. Chambers, Tonya D. Clayton, Mark R. Hafen, Gary T. Mitchum. *Sea Level Rise in Florida.* Gainesville: University Press of Florida, 2016.

Hine, Albert C., Ph.D. Professor Emeritus, Department of Marine Science, University of South Florida. Personal Communications, February 2018.

Hodge, Frederick Webb. *Spanish Explorers of the Southern United States 1528–1543.* Austin: Texas State Historical Association, 1990.

Hoffman, Paul E. *A New Andalucía and a Way to the Orient.* Baton Rouge: Louisiana State University Press, 1990.

————. "Narváez and Cabeza de Vaca in Florida." Undated essay in Hudson and Tesser, 1994 [See below].

Hoogenboom, Lynn. *Juan Ponce de León: A Primary Source Biography.* New York: Powerkids Press, 2006

Howse, H. D. "Navigation and Astronomy—I. The First Three Thousand Years." Presidential Address. Greenwich, London: National Maritime Museum, 1981.

Hudson, Charles. *Knights of Spain, Warriors of the Sun.* Athens and London: University of Georgia Press, 1997.

Hudson, Charles M., and Carmen Chávez Tesser. *The Forgotten Centuries: Indians and Europeans in the American South, 1521–1704*. Athens and London: University of Georgia Press, 1994.

Jameson, J. Franklin. *Spanish Explorers in the Southern United States*. New York: Charles Scribner's Sons, 1907 [Edited by Jameson. Contains Buckingham Smith's translations of "Narrative of Alvar Nuñez Cabeza de Vaca" and the "Narrative of the Expedition of Hernando de Soto by the Gentleman of Elvas."] Reprinted by Scholar Select.

Kite-Powell, Rodney and Arthur R. Savage. *Tampa Bay's Waterfront: Its History and Development*. Sarasota: Coastal Printing, 2016.

Kohl, Johann Georg. *A Descriptive Catalogue of Those Maps, Charts and Surveys Relating to America, which are Mentioned in V3 of Hakluyt's Great Works (1857)*. Washington: Henry Polkinhorn, Printer, 1857.

————. *A Popular History of the Discovery of America*. London: Chapman and Hall, 1862.

————. *Die Beiden Ältesten General-Karten von Amerika Ausgeführt in den Jahren 1527 und 1529*. Weimar: Geographisches Institut, 1860. [Includes unbound copies of 1527 and 1529 *Carta Universal* of the *Casa de Contratación*, Seville]

————. *History of Discovery and Exploration on the Coasts of the United States. Appendix No. 19.1885*. Reprinted by Kessinger's Rare Reprints. Undated.

Krock, Jennifer Rose. "Historical Morphodynamics of John's Pass, West-Central Florida." Graduate Thesis and Dissertation. University of South Florida. Scholar Commons, 2005.

Lavender, David. *DeSoto, Coronado, Cabrillo: Explorers of the Northern Mystery*. Washington, D. C.: Division of Publications, National Park Service, U.S. Department of the Interior, 1992.

Lester, Toby. *The Fourth Part of the World*. New York: Free Press, 2009.

Long, Haniel. *Interlinear to Cabeza de Vaca*. Santa Fe, New Mexico: Writers' Editions, 1936.

————. *The Marvelous Adventures of Cabeza de Vaca*. Clearlake, California: The Dawn Horse Press, 1992.

Loker, Aleck. *La Florida: Spanish Exploration & Settlement in North America, 1500 to 1600*.Williamsburg, VA: Solitude Press, 2010.

Lowery, Woodbury. *A Descriptive List of Maps of the Spanish Possessions within the Present Limits of the United States, 1502–1820*. Washington, D.C.: Government Printing Office, 1912.

————. *The Spanish Settlements Within the Present Limits of the United States, 1513–1561*. New York, 1905. (Reprinted. Reink Books, 2017.)

Lyon, Eugene. *The Enterprise of Florida: Pedro Menéndez de Avilés and Spanish Conquest of 1565-1568*. Gainesville: University Press of Florida, 1974 and 1976.

MacDougald, James E. *The Pánfilo de Narváez Expedition of 1528*. St. Petersburg, FL: Marsden House, 2018.

Martyr d'Anghiera, Peter. See Anghiera, Peter Martyr d'.

McGoun, William E. *Prehistoric Peoples of South Florida*. Tuscaloosa and London: The University of Alabama Press, 1993.

Merás, Luisa Martín. *Cartografía Marítima Hispana: La imagen de América*. Madrid: Lunwerg Editores. [undated].

Michaels, Will. *The Making of St. Petersburg*. Charleston, S.C. : The History Press, 2012.

Milanich, Jerald. *Florida Indians and the Invasion from Europe*. Gainesville: University Press of Florida, 1995.

———. *The Timucua*. Oxford, UK: Blackwell Publishers, 1996.

Mitchem, Jeffrey M. *The West and Central Florida Expeditions of Clarence Bloomfield Moore*. Tuscaloosa: University of Alabama Press, 1999.

Montero, Juan Gomez. Fundación Nao Victoria. Seville, Spain. Personal Communication. February 2018.

Moore, Clarence Bloomfield. *Certain Aboriginal Mounds of the Florida Central West Coast (1903)*. [Undated. Kessinger Legacy Reprints.]

Myers, Kathleen Anne. *Fernando de Oviedo's Chronicle of America*. Austin: University of Texas Press, 2007.

National Oceanic and Atmospheric Administration. Office of Coastal Survey. Charts 11412, 11425, 11426. Web. 2018.

Navarette, Martin Fernández. *Colección de los viajes y descubrimientos que hicieron por mas los españoles desde fines del siglio XV, con varios documentos inéditos concernientes á la historia de la marina castellana y dos los establecimientos españoles en Indias*. Madrid: Imprenta Real, 1825. [archive.org/details/coleccibonviages04navarich]

Nordenskiöld, A. E. *Facsimile-Atlas to the Early History of Cartography with Reproductions of the Most Important Maps*

Printed in the XV and XVI Centuries. Stockholm: 1889. (Dover Edition—New York: Dover Publications, Inc., 1973.)

Núñez Cabeza de Vaca, Álvar. *The Account: Álvar Núñez Cabeza de Vaca's* Relación. Translated and annotated by Martin A. Favata and José B. Fernández. Houston: Arte Publico Press, 1993.

————. *A Cabeza de Vaca Book.* Translated by Fanny Bandelier. Edited by Doyle Phillips. Contains reproductions of each page of 1555 *Relación*. 250 copies printed. Doyle Phillips/ Fotografica, 1999.

————. *The Account of Cabeza de Vaca.* Translated by David Carson. Friendswood, Texas: Living Water Specialties, 2018.

————. *Álvar Núñez Cabeza de Vaca: Chronicle of the Narváez Expedition.* Translated by Fanny Bandelier. Revised and annotated by Harold Augenbaum. New York Penguin Books, 2002.

————. *Cabeza de Vaca's Adventures in the Unknown Interior of America.* Translated by Cyclone Covey. Albuquerque: University of New Mexico Press, 1983.

————. *Castaways: The Narrative of Álvar Núñez Cabeza de Vaca.* Translated by Frances M. López-Morillas. Ed. and introduction by Enríque Pupo-Walker. Berkeley, Los Angeles, and London: University of California Press, 1993.

————. *The Journey and Ordeal of Cabeza de Vaca.* Translated and edited by Cyclone Covey. Mineola, New York: Dover Publications, 1961.

————. *The Journey of Alvar Nuñez Cabeza de Vaca.* Translated by Fanny Bandelier. Chicago: The Rio Grande Press, 1964.

————. *La relacion que dio Aluar nuñez cabeça de vaca de lo acaescido en las Indias en la armada donde yua por gouernador Panphilo de narbaez desde el año de veynte y siete hasta el año de treynta y seis que boluio a Seuilla con tres de sus compañia.* Zamora, 1542.

————. *La relacion y comentarios del gouernador Aluar nuñez cabeça de vaca, de lo acaescido en las dos jornados que hizo a las Indias.* Valladolid, 1555.

————. *The Narrative of Alvar Nuñez Cabeça de Vaca.* Translated by Buckingham Smith. Washington, 1851

————. *Naufragios de Álvar Nuñez Cabeça de Vaca y Relación de la jornada que hizo a la Florida con el Adelantado Pánfilo de Narváez.* Ed. Enrique de Vedía. *Biblioteca de Autores Españoles.* Vol. 22. Madrid: Imprenta y Estereotipía de M. Rivadeneyra, 1852.

————. *The Narrative of Alvar Núñez Cabeza de Vaca.* Translated by Fanny Bandelier. Barre, Massachusetts: The Imprint Society, 1972. [Also contains *Oviedo's Version of the Lost Joint Report Presented to the Audiencia of Santo Domingo.* Translated by Gerald Theisen]

————. *The Narrative of Cabeza de Vaca.* Edited and translated by Rolena Adorno and Patrick Charles Pautz. Lincoln and London: University of Nebraska Press, 1999 [See also Adorno, Rolena].

————. *Relación de los naufragios y comentarios de Álvar Núñez Cabeza de vaca.* Vol. 5. *Coleccíon de libros y documentos referents a la historia de América.* Ed. Manuel Serrano y Sanz. Madrid: Librería General de Victoriano Suárez, 1906.

————. *Relation of Alvar Nuñez Cabeça de Vaca*. Translated by Buckingham Smith. New York 1871. (Reprinted by Cornell University Library. Digital Collections, Undated.)

Ober, Frederick Albion. *Juan Ponce de León*. New York and London: Harper & Brothers Publishing, 1908. (Facsimile edition by Scholar Select. Undated.)

Otterness, Anders. "*Cabeza de Vaca and Estevanico*." Ph.D. dissertation. U.C. Santa Cruz, 2002.

Oviedo y Valdés, Gonzalo Fernández. *Historia General Y Natural De Las Indias: Islas Y Tierrafirme Del Mar Oceano*. Primary Source Edition. Madrid 1853. Published in U.S. in 1932. Reprinted by NABU Public Domain Reprints. (Obtained from University of Texas Library.) Undated.

————. *Misfortunes and Shipwrecks in the Seas of the Indies, Islands, and Mainland of the Ocean Sea (1513–1548)*. Translation by Glen F. Dille of Book Fifty of the General and Natural History of the Indies by Gonzalo Fernández de Oviedo. Tallahassee: University Press of Florida, 2011.

————. *The Expedition of Pánfilo de Narváez*. Translation by Gerald Theisen of Book XXXV, Chapters 1–6 of Historia General y Natural de las Indias, Islas, y Tierra-Firme del Mar Oceano. [Oviedo's summary of the Joint Report] Albuquerque: Gerald Theisen, 1974 . Also found in *The Narrative of Alvar Núñez Cabeza de Vaca*. Translated by Fanny Bandelier. Barre, Massachusetts: The Imprint Society, 1972.

Padgen, Anthony. *Hernán Cortés: Letters from Mexico*. New Haven and London: Yale University Press, 1986.

Padrón, Ricardo. "Charting Empire, Charting Difference: Gómara's *Historia general de las Indias* and Spanish Maritime Cartography." *Colonial Latin America Review*, Vol. 11, No. 1, 2002. pp. 47–69.

――――. *The Spacious World*. Chicago and London: The University of Chicago Press, 2004.

Parish, Helen Rand. *Bartolomé de las Casas: The Only Way*. New York and Mahwah, N. J.: Paulist Press, 1992.

Peet, Steven Denison. *The American Antiquarian and Oriental Journal*. F. H. Revnell. 1899. (Reprinted by Ulan Press, 2016).

Pérez-Mallaína, Pablo E. *Spain's Men of the Sea: Daily Life on the Indies Fleets in the Sixteenth Century*. Baltimore and London: The Johns Hopkins University Press, 1998.

Perry, I. Mac, *Indian Mounds You Can Visit*. St. Petersburg, FL: Great Outdoors Publishing Company, 1993.

Phillips, Doyle. *A Cabeza de Vaca Book*. Translated by Fanny Bandelier. Edited by Doyle Phillips. Contains reproductions of each page of 1555 *Relación*. 250 copies printed. Doyle Phillips/Fotografica, 1999.

Phinney, A. H. "Narváez and Hernando de Soto: Their Landing Places and the Town of Espiritu Santo." *Florida Historical Quarterly* (Jan. 1925: pp. 15–21).

Pike, Dag. *The History of Navigation*. South Yorkshire, England: Pen & Sword Books Ltd, 2018.

Ptolemy, Claudius. *Cosmography*. Introduction by Lelio Pagani. Leicester, England: Magna Books, 1990.

――――. *Geography of Claudius Ptolemy*. Translated by Edward Luther Stevenson. New York: Cosmo Classics, 2011.

Reinhartz, Dennis, and Gerald D. Saxon. *The Mapping of the Entradas into the Greater Southwest*. Norman: University of Oklahoma Press, 1998.

Reséndez, Andrés. *A Land So Strange*. New York: Basic Books, 2007.

Sandman, Alison. "Spanish Nautical Cartography in the Renaissance." *The History of Cartography*. Volume Two. Chicago: The University of Chicago Press, 1987.

Santos-Granero, Fernando. *Vital Enemies*. Austin: University of Texas Press, 2009.

Schneider, Paul. *Brutal Journey: The Epic Story of the First Crossing of North America*. New York: Henry Holt and Company, 2006.

Sheppard, Donald E. *The Conquest of North America by Hernando de Soto, Coronado, and Cabeza de Vaca*. Ebook. Floridahistory.com. Undated.

Simpson, Terrance L. *The Narváez /Anderson Site (8Pi54): A Safety Harbor Culture Shell Mound and Midden—AD 1000– 1600*. Central Gulf Coast Archaeological Society, 1998.

Smith, Roger C. *Vanguard of Empire: Ships of Exploration in the Age of Columbus*. New York—Oxford: Oxford University Press, 1993.

Stevenson, Edward Luther. *A Description of Early Maps, Originals and Facsimiles (1492–1611) Being a Part of the Wall Exhibition of the American Geographical Society*. New York City: The American Geographical Society, 1913.

———. *Early Spanish Cartography of the New World with Special Reference to the Wolfenbüttel Map and the Work of Diego Ribero.* Worcester, Mass: American Antiquarian Society, 1909.

————. "Maps Illustrating Early Discovery and Exploration in America." [Reprinted from The American Historical Review. Vol. 8. No. 4. 4 July 1905.]

————. *Typical Early Maps of the New World.* Vol. 39. E.L. Stevenson: 1907.

Terrell, John Upton. *Journey into Darkness.* New York: William Morrow & Co., 1962.

Theisen, Gerald. *The Expedition of Pánfilo de Narváez.* Translation by Gerald Theisen of Book XXXV, Chapters 1-6 of *Historia General y Natural de las Indias, Islas, y Tierra-Firme del Mar Oceano.* [Oviedo's summary of the Joint Report]. Albuquerque: Gerald Theisen, 1974.

Thomson, Bailey. "In Search of Spanish Pathways." Essay appearing in *Spanish Pathways in Florida*, Ed. by Ann L. Henderson and Gary Mormino. Sarasota, FL: Pineapple Press, 1991 (pp. 24–31).

Tooley, R. V. *Maps and Map-Makers.* New York: Dorset Press, 1990.

Torello, Joan Carlos Oliver. "A Spy, a Map, and the Quest for Power in 16th Century Europe." *National Geographic History Magazine.* April 2017.

Todd, Millicent. *Peru: A Land of Contrasts.* Boston: Little Brown and Company, 1914.

Turrell, Todd and Brian Schmidt. *The Florida Keys: A History Through Maps.* Naples, Florida: Island Map Publishing, LLC, [2020].

Van Cittert, P. H. *Astrolabes*. Leiden: E.J. Brill, 1954.

Varnum, Robin. *Álvar Núñez Cabeza de Vaca*. Norman: University of Oklahoma Press, 2014.

Vega, Garcialaso de la. *The Florida of the Inca*. Translated and edited by John Grier Garner and Jeannette Johnson Varner. Austin: University of Texas Press, 1951.

Virga, Vincent, and Lynne E. Wright. *Florida—Mapping the Sunshine State Through History*. Guilford, CT: Morris Book Publishing, 2011.

Wagner, Henry R. *Antonio de Herrera*. Berkeley: 1924.

Wang, Ping, Ph.D. Professor, Department of Geology, University of South Florida. Personal Communications, February 2018. Also, Appendix III.

Ware, John D. *George Gauld: Surveyor and Cartographer of the Gulf Coast*. Gainesville -Tampa: The University Presses of Florida, 1982.

Weddle, Robert. *Spanish Sea: The Gulf of Mexico in North American Discovery, 1500-1653*. College Station, Texas: Texas A&M University Press, 1985.

Wiles, Kate. "The Map: Tenochtitlan, 1524." *History Today*. (Vol. 66, Issue 10. October 2016).

Willey, *Archaeology of the Florida Gulf Coast*. Gainesville: University Press of Florida, 2016.

Williams, John Lee. *The Territory of Florida*. New York: HT Goodrich, 1837. (Reprinted London: Forgotten Books, 2012).

Williams, Lindsey Wilger. *Boldly Onward – A True History Mystery Related to the Incredible Adventures of America's "Adelantados" and Clues to Their Landing Places in Florida.* Charlotte Harbor, Florida: Precision Publishing, 1986.

Wilson-Lee, Edward. *The Catalogue of Shipwrecked Books.* New York: Scribner, 2020.

Winsor, Justin. *The Kohl Collection (Now in the Library of Congress) of Maps Relating to America.* Washington: Government Printing Office, 1904.

Wolf, Hans. *America: Early Maps of the New World.* Munich: Prestel. 1992.

Wood, Peter. *The Spanish Main.* Alexandria, VA: Time-Life Books, 1979.

Worth, John E. *Discovering Florida: First Contact Narratives from Spanish Expeditions along the Lower Gulf Coast.* Gainesville: University Press of Florida, 2014.

———. "The Settlement of Spanish Florida." Faculty Homepage. University of West Florida. Undated.

Index

Made in United States
Orlando, FL
03 October 2023

37529201R00214